A HAUNTED HISTORY
OF
LOUISIANA PLANTATIONS

CHERYL H. WHITE, PhD, AND W. RYAN SMITH, MA

Haunted America

Published by Haunted America
A Division of The History Press
www.historypress.net

Back cover, inset: Houmas House Plantation at Burnside, Louisiana. *Library of Congress, Prints and Photographs Division, Historic American Buildings Survey.*

First published 2017

Manufactured in the United States

ISBN 9781626198753

Library of Congress Control Number: 2017940958

CONTENTS

Acknowledgements

There are many people, places and agencies that helped make this work possible and to whom we owe special gratitude. Thanks to the history majors and graduate students of Louisiana State University at Shreveport, especially Mitchell Baxter, Ashley Dean, Catherine Green, Joanna Hunt and Ciara Mathis. A special thanks also goes to Bess Maxwell and Connie Williamson of Louisiana Spirits for their assistance with some of the paranormal aspects of this book.

Much gratitude is owed to the people interviewed for this work in gathering the oral histories, legends and folklore of these beguiling Louisiana plantations, including Mr. Dustin Fuqua, Judge Henley Hunter, Mr. Tommy Whitehead, Mr. Jim Blanchard, Mr. Kevin Kelly and those tour guides we will forever know by first name only. They gave the most precious resource possible for our sake: their own time.

There are also institutions that merit acknowledgement, including Cane River Creole National Historical Park, the Association for the Preservation of Historic Natchitoches, the San Francisco Plantation Foundation and the River Road Historical Society. The Noel Library at Louisiana State University at Shreveport provided resources and inter-library loan support, as did the library of Tulane University in New Orleans.

We are grateful to the tireless staff of The History Press, especially our editor, Candice Lawrence.

Finally, we would like to extend a special note of gratitude to mutual friend Father Peter Mangum for making the introduction that began a fun and fascinating collaboration!

CHAPTER 1
"IN HOUSES WHICH ARE OLD"

A PRIMER TO THE LOUISIANA BIG HOUSE

In houses which are old—the forms of whose very walls and pillars have taken body from the thoughts of men in a vanished time—we often sense something far more delicate, more unwordable, than the customary devices of the romanticist: the swish of a silken invisible dress on stairs once dustless, the fragrance of an unseen blossom of other years, the wraith momentarily given form in a begrimed mirror. These wordless perceptions can be due only, it seems, to something still retained in these walls; something crystalized from the energy of human emotion and the activities of human nerves.
—*Clarence John Laughlin, author,* Ghosts Along the Mississippi

The landscape of Louisiana today is dotted with visible reminders of a long-lost age, particularly in those areas along the old arterial rivers of the state. The age of the great plantation echoes across more than a lifetime of separation, with profound cultural and historical impacts that once wrought the state's identity from the primitive colonial past and continue to shape its character today. The fabled antebellum period throughout the Deep South was home to an economic system that would quickly pass into the pages of history, but not without leaving behind a rich and intriguing narrative.

After the Civil War, the plantation estate remained for a time—evolving, flexing, straining but not breaking until it was at last vanquished by mechanized farming through the slow and strangling death of the last great holdouts to the Industrial Revolution. That resulting heritage, this residue of the agrarian country estates, the enslaved families, those peeling façades and crumbling pillars contain a shared memory that perpetuates still. The plantation encounter today is framed within the context of a distinctively original folklore—occasionally light and interesting, often mysterious and dark but universally compelling. There is in them something at once horrific and grand, something both pure and irreverent, both stately and remote, something uniquely Louisianan.

It is through that colorful lens of haunted folklore that this work seeks to tell some familiar history in a new way. Scattered throughout the plantation chronicles of Louisiana are tales of ghosts said to haunt stately mansions, evidence of lively superstitions of both slave and free populations. There are vestiges of fascinating social reactions indicative of a bygone era, all of which frame a way of life that breathed its last as the cacophony of the petroleum-powered farm-all tore open the alluvium in neatly furrowed lanes. Certainly, there are many footprints through time that shape this particularly unique journey of Louisiana history, most of which are rooted in the very land itself, with both ancient and contemporary cultural influences.

Long before the Europeans set eyes on Louisiana, the vast wilderness of marshy swamps and bayous throughout the south and deep timber forests of the north was home to Paleo-Amerindians. The now-identified major tribes of the Caddo, Tunica, Natchez, Atakapa, Choctaw, Houma and Natchez settled the region millennia before Sieur de La Salle claimed all the lands drained by the great Mississippi River in the name of French King Louis XIV in 1682. There can be no question that their culture, even in assimilation with that of new peoples, would leave an imprint on the future. Throughout much of the French colonial period in Louisiana, the native population far outnumbered the European *expatrié*. Yet with inevitable conquest and colonization, the unique civilizations of these ancient people were threatened to near-extinction. Soon enough, the arrival of the French, Spanish and African peoples would gradually but dramatically transform the subsistence farming and nomadic lifestyles and small-scale farming of the natives into a much larger and commercially successful agricultural economy.

Colonial authorities issued grants of large sections of land in Louisiana (concessions) to people of already distinguished wealth and influence. These earliest Europeans would produce a distinct class known as *Creoles*—those born in Louisiana of either French or Spanish descent—while intermarriage with Africans would beget the *Creoles of Color*. Many people settling in the new territory of Louisiana received smaller plots of land known as *habitations*, usually only a few acres, which were gradually consolidated by agreement into larger farms. With the passage of time and influence of new technologies, both of these kinds of land grants resulted in the development of what would become a plantation system, distinguished from farms primarily by sheer acreage and gross crop production. These were truly for-profit enterprises. While many people believe that such plantations were always characterized by large stately mansions surrounded by thousands of acres of rich land, this is not really an accurate depiction of the typical planter's built environment. Most dwellings were not as grand as popular culture has portrayed them to be, but of those that were, the surviving ones are nothing short of wonders. These houses form the crux of the "mystifying landscape" of planter society. Louisiana is fortunate to have many diverse examples.

Under these conditions, the migration patterns of Europeans to Louisiana merged with an existing native culture and then was further augmented by the arrival of the Africans. Because Louisiana was first a French colony, then Spanish, then French again, due to the complexities of war and treaty transfers, the territory was unique from most of the remainder of what would become the United States in at least one significant way. With the exception of a brief occupation of a few southeastern parishes, Louisiana was never a wholly British colony. This meant that the cultural mix of Louisiana was destined to be different from surrounding states and even the remainder of the emerging nation.

In addition, Louisiana's geography and topography was marvelously original. Being home to some of the most extensive wetlands in the United States means that large portions of the state are marshy, if not completely under water. As the drainage basin of the fourth largest river in the world, the Mississippi delta region features a complex network of rivers and bayous that originally were not only water sources for the populations of both natives and settlers but also major highways of transportation in a thick wilderness. All of this contributes to an emerging cultural composite that would distinctly frame Louisiana's history. There is perhaps no greater living expression of this uniqueness than the Louisiana plantation landscape.

After meager successes in tobacco and indigo, the first major cash crop of Louisiana was sugar cane, although this did not become particularly profitable or widespread until the early nineteenth century. Trial and error mostly characterized Louisiana's earliest efforts to produce sugar beginning in the 1750s, in a desperate attempt to match the ever-rising European demand for the tropical crop. As Caribbean natives began to come to Louisiana, they brought a new variety of sugar, and while more suited to the climate, it was also not successful on a large scale. Not until the early 1800s did Louisiana begin to consistently produce sugar, and once news of the crop's success began to spread, more and more lands throughout the southern regions of the state were converted to its production. On the eve of the Civil War, Louisiana was producing approximately half of the sugar that was consumed in the United States. Today, some of the old sugar cane plantations of Louisiana are storied and stable reminders of the still important place that agricultural production plays, even in a now global market.

By the second quarter of the nineteenth century, cotton had become another significant cash crop grown in a large plantation setting. Again, it required agricultural innovation to make this possible. In the case of cotton, it was Eli Whitney's 1793 invention of the cotton gin (short for engine) that was responsible for a farming revolution. By the time the Civil War broke out in 1861, Louisiana was producing approximately one-sixth of the nation's cotton and was responsible for the largest share of cotton exported to Europe. Unlike sugar, which tended to be exclusively a large-scale plantation crop, many smaller farms in Louisiana also grew cotton, with fewer resources and laborers.

Centrally important to supporting a plantation economy was, of course, the harsh reality of slave labor. Sugar and cotton were both labor-intensive crops until later improvements in machine agricultural technology came along in the twentieth century. This meant that large numbers of laborers were necessary in the plantation system, most of whom were provided by African slaves, often imported by way of the Caribbean and major ports in the southern United States. The self-sufficiency of major plantations, along with their relative isolation from one another, meant that they became communities unto themselves with local customs and traditions based on a shared institutional history. The lore associated with these communities originates within just such a context; it is the isolation of a local culture that finds expression in the tales that have been handed down.

The scope of an undertaking such as this is necessarily limited by the fact that Louisiana has preserved a great deal of its plantation history. Many of the state's original plantation homes and some associated structures still exist. In a few rarer and more remote examples, entire plantation cultural landscapes remain largely intact. Poverty, rather than wealth, is historic preservation's first friend. In total, those places that have been designated National Historic Landmarks or placed in the National Register of Historic Places number well over one hundred, and that is a fraction of what once

Sugar cane workers in Louisiana at the end of the nineteenth century. *Library of Congress, Special Photos Collection.*

existed. Some of these buildings are deteriorating despite efforts to save them, and their landscapes are being swallowed up once more—either by nature reclaiming its own or by suburban sprawl or industrial production. Not all of the survivors are open to the public. The focus of this work is, therefore, directed at admittedly a mere handful of plantations but features those with remarkably resilient folklore that helps tell the history of not only the place but also, importantly, the lives of the people who once lived there. How we interpret these relic landscapes are reflections on how we view ourselves as Louisianans.

There are yet other avenues of exploration available. Anyone intrigued by Louisiana history knows that no surviving plantation is complete without at least one ghost story. This makes for a compelling incentive for tourism, but such stories are also a product of a culture that once perpetuated superstition. Visitors today flock to these places not just to admire the architecture or grand sweeping environs of antebellum homes but also to encounter the past through the lens of the paranormal. In Vacherie, the iconic Oak Alley Plantation is purportedly home to at least four ghosts: that of Jacques Roman, whose family built the home in the 1830s; his wife, Marie; and daughters Josephine and Marie, as well as former slaves. Reports of ghostly apparitions persist, drawing thousands of visitors each year but providing a unique lens through which to focus and retell the incredible history of one of Louisiana's oldest surviving sugar plantations.

Much the same can be said of Houmas House, Nottaway, Edgewood and San Francisco Plantations, to name just a few within the scope of this book. Others, such as Melrose Plantation nestled along the Cane River near Natchitoches, feature histories that truly set them apart in rather unusual ways. Melrose was built by and for free people of color, which would be remarkable enough, but it was also home to famed twentieth-century folk artist Clementine Hunter. It is not hard to imagine that Melrose would produce a compelling lore all its own, including the fortune that spared Melrose from the fires of the Union army that destroyed many other Natchitoches-area homes and structures.

The traditional stories produced within communities are at the heart of folklore. This differs from the discipline of history, chiefly because folklore both derives and departs from the written record. A critical characteristic of folklore demands that it be passed down from generation to generation through oral tradition, and the stories explored herein rise to that challenge.

CHAPTER 2

The Gentlemen by the River

HOUMAS HOUSE

In the present time, what once was has a mystical quality. Here, under the shade of massive oaks draped in lichen and laced in memories, there are sprawling and fragrant gardens. The stories about the big house they shelter and beautify are fascinating and indicative of unexpected allure in the shadow of the altogether obvious grandeur. In the Louisiana moonlight, the trees themselves are illuminated as specters of an era that has long since passed away. Indeed, there once were many more, but those that remain hold fast to the mystical legends of Houmas House. It is said that one of the plantation's owners named the oaks "The Gentlemen." Throughout the years, they have been known to personify human emotions over events affecting the place and its history. Here, there is a connection between flora and southern heritage strong enough to make a Natchez magnolia blush. There are intriguing tales to summon from the pages of documented history, but let the traveler begin with what the senses can readily assess.

William Howard Russell, an English journalist who visited Houmas House in 1860 while reporting for the *London Times*, summarizes almost exactly the first impression any traveler might have today:

> *An avenue lined with trees and branches close set, drooping and overarching a walk paved with red brick, led to the house, the porch of which was visible at the extremity of the lawn with clustering flowers, rose, jessamine, and creepers clinging to the pillars, supporting the verandah. The view from the belvedere on the roof was one of the most striking of its kind in the world.*[1]

The impressive grounds not only feature the Classical Revival mansion known today as Houmas House but also boast an original small house from the late eighteenth century, as well as the strikingly interesting *garçonnières* that reflect the French colonial desire for separate housing of young men of the family once they reached adolescence.[2] While Russell's account appeared in print before the plantation became graced with the many specters that roam its halls today, his description is nevertheless just as relevant. The view from Houmas House looking toward the Mississippi River remains, as Russell noted, "one of the most striking of its kind in the world." The witness of the moss-draped trees extends far into the past, before the arrival of European settlers to Louisiana, long before there were sugar cane plantations lining the Mississippi River and before the land would have recognized anything but the now-foreign language of a native tongue. The structures built by sugar barons only anchor the ground that once belonged to the Houmas Indians, and it is with them that the history of Louisiana's noted "sugar palace" truly begins.

The Houmas tribe first began to settle the area in the late seventeenth century, and French explorer LaSalle mentions them in his 1682 journal log. By 1699, their presence was also noted by Sieur de Bienville. Their settlement was expansive along the river, as ongoing archaeological discoveries attest. Hostilities between the French and the English that rocked the continent of Europe inevitably spilled over into the New World and drove the Houmas farther south into modern-day Louisiana.[3] In 1774, the Houmas chieftain Colabee sold a plot of land near the riverbank to investors Alexandre Latil, originally of Paris, France, and Maurice Conway, who was born in Limerick, Ireland, and was a nephew of Alexandro O'Reilly. The sale deed records that the men received the land from the Houmas in exchange for goods worth $150, including copper pots, weapons, sugar and mirrors.[4] Latil is credited with building the first structure on the property, a simple four-room house that came to be known simply as the "French House," and then sold his interests to Conway the following year. It appears that the Houmas remained in the area for at least another decade, by which time further European expansion was underway.[5]

With the turn of the nineteenth century, the explosion of sugar cane as a viable crop transformed the lands and its culture. From that point forward, the history of Houmas House is steeped in the intrigue and political saga of Louisiana's richest sugar barons. Legal battles and property disputes dominate the narrative of the early owners, a testimony to the high stakes of the industry and the wealth it produced.

Houmas House, the "Sugar Palace," near Burnside, Louisiana. *Courtesy of Houmas House.*

In 1805, Daniel Clark acquired the Houmas land. He was the first to represent the Territory of Orleans in the United States House of Representatives and was also the first to introduce the cultivation of sugar cane to the Houmas lands. Clark had a provocative and interesting personal life, outwardly living in New Orleans society as a bachelor yet was all the while legally married to Zulime Carriere, with a daughter (Myra) by the marriage born in 1806. In 1811, Clark sold the sugar cane lands to Revolutionary War hero General Wade Hampton for $300,000. Included in the sale were two hundred slaves. By this time, Hampton was the top military official for the United States Territory of Orleans and had already amassed great wealth from his previous landholdings in South Carolina.

Clark died in 1813, just two years after selling the Houmas property to Hampton, and left behind a personal estate estimated to be worth millions of dollars. In addition to his wealth, part of Clark's legacy proved to be an estate controversy. There were reported to be two versions of his last will and testament, hotly contested in the courts, due to an inheritance claim placed by Clark's "secret child."[6]

Myra Clark Gaines claimed that Daniel Clark had actually executed a second will in 1813, superseding the one of 1811 that had named only his business associates as his heirs. Myra claimed the second will (naming her as sole beneficiary and acknowledging her as Clark's legitimate heir) had been deliberately destroyed by those who would benefit from the 1811 version. The case was litigated in probate for decades, finally reaching the jurisdiction of the United States Supreme Court, which decided in Myra's favor in 1884. Unfortunately, the victory came years after her death. By the time Myra Clark Gaines's heirs were recognized as the lawful claimants to Clark's original fortune, most of it was gone. Interestingly, legal battles seem to punctuate the early history of Houmas House plantation, since the long-running Clark lawsuit is matched in United States history only by that of future owner Wade Hampton, who sued to obtain ownership of adjacent Houmas lands.[7] This also proved to be a legal battle that lasted many years, challenging the emerging understandings of public lands law, as well as pitting large sugar plantation owners against smaller farming interests and "squatters" who simply moved in as the new territory was opened under United States jurisdiction.

Therefore, Houmas House is actually at the center of two of the longest-running legal battles in the history of American civil jurisprudence. The second example, the so-called Houmas Claim of 1845, involved General Wade Hampton and other major sugar planters along the Mississippi River. The origins of this protracted land dispute reached back to the time of the original owners of Conway and Latil, who in 1806 made a claim with the registrar of the Public Land Office showing property boundaries that extended to the Amite River and Lake Maurepas, far beyond what the United States government allowed on "backlands" adjacent to property acquired either by colonial grant or previous purchase from the natives. The Public Land Office wrestled with questions over jurisdiction and the extent of the law as, meanwhile, other settlers began coming to the area, moving into the backlands and also taking advantage of the opportunity to purchase public lands.[8] These lands were often in dispute because they were simultaneously claimed by the prominent sugar planters, and this inevitably led to legal actions that lasted until 1884. The courts finally held that the original claimants had no legitimate ownership of lands beyond what had been originally acknowledged, which the United States Congress had long held since the earliest land grant acts governing public lands.[9] Even in its eventual defeat, the Houmas Claim is a notable and powerful reminder of the influence of the sugar owners along the Mississippi River.

Wade Hampton's daughter Caroline married John Preston of South Carolina, and they are responsible for the construction of the existing house, a magnificent Greek Revival edifice completed in 1828. During this time, about 1840, the two signature *garçonnières* were built on the formal front lawns,

Houmas House, front elevation showing original cistern. *Library of Congress, Prints and Photographs Division, Historic American Buildings Survey.*

adjacent to each side of the main mansion. They are beautifully ornamental additions, two-story, hexagonal in shape, standing over thirty feet high.[10] The buildings speak directly to the heavy influence that French colonial ideas still held over this part of Louisiana, even into the mid-nineteenth century.

The property passed next to John Burnside in 1857, and by that time, it included Houmas House and twelve thousand acres of sugar cane. Houmas House became only one of a vast network of plantations that Burnside owned, including nearby Riverton, which was lost in the 1960s due to river encroachment and levee work. On the eve of the Civil War, Burnside was easily the wealthiest sugar planter in the region and highly influential, evidenced by the fact that he was able to effectively declare his "immunity" to Union occupation because he was technically a citizen of Great Britain.[11] The maneuver worked, as Houmas House came through the war unscathed, unoccupied and unmolested, with its lands and crops intact. Burnside notably also renewed with vigor Wade Hampton's part in the original Houmas Claim.

Above: A *garçonnière* at Houmas House. *Library of Congress, Prints and Photographs Division, Historic American Buildings Survey.*

Left: A *garçonnière* with majestic live oak trees at Houmas House. *Library of Congress, Prints and Photographs Division, Historic American Buildings Survey.*

An architectural rendering of a *garçonnière* at Houmas House. *Library of Congress, Prints and Photographs Division, Historic American Buildings Survey.*

Houmas House became the property of William Porcher Miles in 1881, following the death of John Burnside. His ignorance of sugar cane farming was soon overcome by his self-study of colonial sugar king Valcour Aime's journals and notes. Following his death in 1899, Houmas House sat vacant and fell into disrepair until 1940, when it was purchased by Dr. George Crozat. Crozat not only restored the built environment but also focused on reimagining the once lush gardens that the plantation was known for in the antebellum period.[12] Today, the plantation and grounds have been even further renewed, restored and expanded under the ownership of Kevin Kelly, who acquired Houmas House in 2003.

Visitors today are confronted with a unique blend of Old South and modern innovation. In addition to the original structures, which have been lovingly preserved, there are new cottage accommodations for overnight guests on the grounds. The once renowned gardens are again in full and splendorous bloom and in every season offer something for the senses. The centuries-old live oaks are fastidiously cared for. Besides those who come with planned purpose, more than an occasional traveler along the River Road is drawn in spontaneously to Houmas House to explore. It is a naturally inviting landscape and one that visibly expresses some of the most unusual folklore to be found in the area. For besides its rich history, the plantation has some prominent supernatural elements associated with it, which has even attracted the attention of national television productions such as *Ghost Hunters* and never fails to ignite the imaginations of those who hear its stories.

The first such tale involves the famous live oak trees on the property. Before the levee was constructed, at least twenty-four trees formed an *allée* that ran to the river's edge. It is repeated in the oral tradition of the plantation that the trees all seemed to grow in such a way as to link their arms in welcome to all who approached the grounds from the Mississippi River—that is, until such time as the River Road altered the landscape. Owner John Burnside referred to the original twenty-four oaks as "The Gentlemen," seeing in them a life force that expressed the very personality of the plantation itself.

Their supernatural legend begins with the Great Mississippi River Flood of 1927, which left much of the surrounding area heavily damaged while Houmas House was spared due to its position on higher ground. In the decade that followed, the Great Depression spawned many engineering projects under the direction of the Works Progress Administration (WPA) as part of a national economic recovery program. One undertaking of the WPA was new and higher levee construction along the River Road area.

By this time, Houmas House was no longer occupied and was falling into disrepair. As the levee was raised, many of "The Gentlemen" fell to the saws and axes of workers. Legend has it that sixteen dishonest workers, intending to profit from the sale of the massive oaks to a nearby mill, perished trying to float the tree trunks past a dangerous bend in the river.

The legend continues that the remaining eight oak trees reshaped themselves into the personification of grief, with their majestic boughs bending all the way to the ground and many of the largest top branches bowed over as if hanging their heads in sorrow. Nearby residents noted the overnight change in the structure of the oaks, something that is readily apparent to any visitor to the grounds even today. The locals still insist that the trees are inhabited by spirits of grief—either those of remorseful workers who perished after destroying the other "Gentlemen" or those of the trees themselves. The twisted and almost-grotesque shape of the oaks today naturally lends itself to such a legend, but in this case, it is one that is richly documented in oral tradition of the area.

Houmas House today reports another prominent legend involving the ghost of a little girl that is said to haunt the house and grounds. When

"The Gentlemen," ancient live oak trees at Houmas House Plantation and the subject of rich folklore. *Courtesy of Houmas House.*

restoration began on the mansion in 2003, electricians reported seeing a young girl, age seven to ten years, dressed in a long blue gown, who descended a stairway and was later seen in the central hall. They all expressed concern to the new owner about the unsafe conditions for a child to be playing about, but of course, there was no child living there. Work resumed, and there were no future sightings until the house was opened for tourists. From time to time, people still report seeing a little girl on the stairwell, matching the same description given by the workers. The history of the house suggests that the little girl might be the restless spirit of the Prestons' young daughter, May, who died of yellow fever shortly after the family moved back to South Carolina in the mid-nineteenth century.

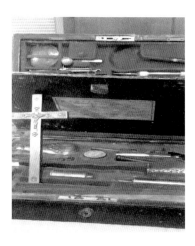

A nineteenth-century "vampire-killing kit." On display at Houmas House today, it represents the superstition of a bygone era. *Photograph by Cheryl H. White.*

Interestingly, the current owner, Kevin Kelly, acquired through a Preston family auction an antique doll dress with May Preston's date of birth appliqued on it, further tangibly linking the little girl back to Houmas House even today.[13] The other suggested identity is the daughter of William Porcher Miles, who died in 1900 and was buried in the family cemetery. The great levee construction of the 1930s unabashedly displaced the graves of this old family cemetery, and her burial marker, along with many others, was shamefully lost. Some believe her spirit roams Houmas House, sorrowful by the circumstance.

Occasionally, visitors to Houmas House have reported a sighting of a distinguished-looking man in uniform, usually spotted on the home's belvedere overlooking the river. Perhaps a riverboat captain looking to the river? Certainly, as many witnesses across the last two centuries have attested, the views of the Mississippi River from that vantage point are unparalleled. What man of the river wouldn't want the unique perspective that only the belvedere of Houmas House can provide?

Workers and visitors have also reported another male presence seen on the grounds—that of an exceptionally tall and thin African American man who appears unperturbed by contemporary structures and simply walks through walls. The owner reports having found an old photograph showing a man fitting this description as he stepped off the front porch of the home over 150 years ago.[14]

The house today, in addition to its resident haunts, is also a veritable museum of unusual historic artifacts, including items that belonged to the Bonaparte family, certainly appropriate considering the plantation's French origins. Among the most unusual finds on display is a nineteenth-century vampire-killing kit. Unique to that era of American history, particularly in the Deep South, vampire legends were as culturally pervasive as the obsession of the current age with zombies and legends of the undead. Legends about vampires and the means to destroy them were simply an expression of the Victorian age and its own peculiar notions of the supernatural. The fact that an assembled vampire kit even existed speaks to a cultural context that is perhaps lost to the present time but somehow seems fittingly at home within the collection of Houmas House today.

Visiting Houmas House, the sojourner is advised to be prepared to step back into the overwhelming opulence of another age, when the sugar barons ruled the Mississippi River. Yet like all great places of historic significance, here one can expect to find both light and darkness, joy and sorrow, woven in equal measure into the tapestry of time. The great wealth that built this "sugar palace" and many others like it still carries the stain of the reality of human slavery, and the families that dwelled here all experienced tragedy and conflict that no amount of money could ever remedy. The stories of all who lived here are imprinted even today and uniquely expressed in the ongoing fascination all feel toward Houmas House folklore. When approaching the main house and its surrounding thirty-eight acres of gardens, stop first to speak to the remaining "Gentlemen." Then pause to listen to the breezes from the river, upon which are carried the echoes of over three hundred years.

Houmas House
40136 Highway 942
Darrow, LA 70725
(225) 473-9380

CHAPTER 3
OF REBELLION AND RESTITUTION

DESTREHAN PLANTATION

There could hardly ever be enough Spanish moss hanging in the scattered oaks across the front lawn beyond the historic River Road and the Mississippi River levee to hide the looming and chunky colonnaded façade of Destrehan Plantation. The big house is immediately upon anyone seeking it out. There is no scenic *allée*; the paved River Road is just feet away from the steps of the front porch. As such, there is little relief from the sun as it burns down across the white gravel-lined trail from the roadway to the more than 225-year-old house. The old iron gate at the street is not showy; it little resembles anything built before the entrance to a contemporary mansion. Nonetheless, the grandeur of the estate captures the attention and motivates the feet to draw nearer still. It is a rare place that speaks to visitors in such a way. Yet, such as it is, the big house at Destrehan is wedged between commercial enterprises and a massive parish library like an old Creole gentleman at a ball between two overbearing dancers. Through the noisy traffic along the paved, ancient trace, Destrehan still speaks to many. It is notably one of the places most widely believed haunted in the entire state.

Destrehan Plantation's big house is located less than twenty-five miles west of the French Quarter in New Orleans along Louisiana Highway 48 and the north shore of the Mississippi River upstream from New Orleans. Today, the river, or rather the levee, is built up just across the street from the big house—the meandering channel having cut hundreds of feet of footage from the former plantation grounds.

The origins of Destrehan Plantation begin with Robert Antoine Robin de Logny, a French colonist who came to Louisiana sometime before 1758.[15] Robin de Logny's time in Louisiana spanned the intermediate period between the earliest colonial beginnings and the full development of the plantation system that produced fantastic wealth, on the back of slave labor, throughout the colony beginning in the late 1780s. Robin de Logny's rise to prominence in colonial Louisiana was crowned by his service in the colonial militia as a captain of the First Company of the Militia of the Germans, escalated from the acquisition of land and especially with his marriage to the daughter of a large estate colonist.[16] In what would otherwise seem a peculiar title, Robin de Logny's rank in the colonial militia stems from his service as a commander of German immigrants who were encouraged to settle in the area. In time, these families would intermarry and even change the spelling or pronunciation of their names to fully assimilate into Creole French society.[17]

In 1787, Robin de Logny began the construction of a proper manor house on established indigo-producing land located about twenty-five

Destrehan Plantation, view from River Road. *Photograph by W. Ryan Smith.*

miles along the River Road from St. Louis Cathedral in the old city. Construction on the house took about three years to complete. Robin de Logny was reaching the end of his time on earth and resided only a couple of years in the house following its completion, dying in December 1792.[18] The original big house was a classic West Indies–influenced Creole manor house, with two floors, three rooms across and two rooms deep. The main living floor was on the second story, in keeping with the French Creole style. A large double-pitched hip roof with a deep gallery wrapped around the house. Thin collonettes above masonry first-floor columns supported the gallery floor. Little attention was paid to symmetry in window and door openings. The bottom story was constructed of heavy masonry to withstand the flooding that was assumed would eventually overtake the property on occasion.[19]

The next generation at Destrehan began with the union of Robin de Logny's youngest daughter, Marie Claude Celeste, to Jean Noel Destrehan in 1786, bringing about the estate's eventual namesake. This marriage, a classic Louisiana arrangement, joined a pair of the colony's wealthiest families.[20] Jean Noel Destrehan was a native of the Louisiana colony, a Creole, as they became known during the Spanish period and thereafter. Destrehan's father had served in the French marines early in the colony's establishment and by 1746 was appointed by King Louis XIV as the royal treasurer of Louisiana. Jean Noel also came into politics early in life. Though he opposed the 1803 annexation of Louisiana into the United States, he was soon thereafter appointed the deputy mayor of the city of New Orleans, a first for the newly American city. Later, at the time of statehood, Jean Noel helped to write the first state constitution and was elected the state's first U.S. senator by the Louisiana legislature.[21]

The Destrehan family moved into the big house following Robin de Logny's death, Jean Noel having purchased the estate at auction for $21,750.[22] Their marriage was a fruitful one, with fourteen children born of the union. There was likely good reason to add the two adjacent wings, or *garçonnières*, to the original house in 1812.[23] The wings would add much-needed square footage for the large family. Beyond altering the house, Destrehan changed production on the plantation from indigo to sugar cane. Immense wealth would soon follow. Destrehan was respected by many as a man with a mind for business, perhaps most notably by William C.C. Claiborne, U.S. territorial governor of Louisiana, who recalled Destrehan as a remarkable "economist."[24] Under his stewardship, Destrehan Plantation would grow to encompass more than one thousand acres.[25]

Portrait of Jean Noel. *Courtesy of Destrehan Plantation and the River Road Historical Society.*

On January 8, 1811, Charles Delondes, a slave loaned on detached service from his master at a neighboring plantation, took the break in monotonous service as an opportunity to change the course of his life, and others, forever.[26] In a sense, it is an ironic twist of fate that Delondes was reportedly his own master's slave driver. Perhaps through his persuasive persona, or maybe during an extended crisis of conscience, he began conspiring with the other slaves around him to rebel against the French citizens who held them in bondage. The conspirators seized a cache of weapons while laboring on the plantation of Manuel Andre, wounding Andre and killing his son. The group set out immediately toward New Orleans down the River Road, their numbers swelling with runaways as they went. As might be expected, the big houses at the plantations along the way were put to the torch, no doubt seen as the seat of unjust power holding them in bondage. The looting and burning continued for miles, prompting droves of free white families to flee toward the city before them.[27]

Under the cry of "On to New Orleans!" the rebellious slaves headed directly for the city. United States territorial governor William C.C. Claiborne summoned the territorial militia after hearing a series of panicked reports of an armed group of hundreds of slaves marching on the city. The smallest estimate of their numbers reached 180; other reports, greatly exaggerated in panic, brought the numbers to nearly 1,000. Nonetheless, the largest slave rebellion in U.S. history was at hand.[28] While New Orleanians alternately panicked and prepared themselves, Delondes and his men reportedly killed another plantation owner along the road.[29] If true, this likely forced Claiborne's hand from waiting in New Orleans to moving forward to aggressively squelch the rebellion. Further, Claiborne's available resources were swelled due to the U.S. annexation of western Florida with a contingent of regular army troops under the command of future Confederate cavalry officer Colonel Wade Hampton. After two days rampant, for Delondes and his men, the taste of freedom was coming to an end. None other than an extremely embittered Manuel Andre and a mass of armed citizens were following them along the River Road to their rear.[30]

Delondes and his men were surrounded by an armed posse to the west, the Mississippi River to the south, impassable terrain to the north and combined elements of the United States Army and a sizeable volunteer militia to the east. Delondes chose to take on Andre and his band first. The ensuing conflict was, of course, intensely personal. The battle was really more of a massacre. Scores of Delondes's men were killed.[31] It is likely that many escaped into the countryside. For the remainder, their fate was met swiftly and brutally.

About two dozen slaves surrendered to Andre's men. The captured men and women were taken to Destrehan Plantation for a trial and sentence; the verdict was hardly in doubt. A St. Charles Parish judge arrived at Destrehan on January 21, and a jury of all-white landowners, including Jean Noel Destrehan, was assembled for the trial. The defendants balked, some readily confessing their intent to kill. Twenty-one were found guilty of rebellion and murder and were sentenced to death; three were acquitted and freed. Among those condemned were two men from Destrehan Plantation, Gross Lindor and Petite Lindor. The men were shot at each of their respective plantations by the militia, probably in full view of the other enslaved workers. When they expired, their corpses were decapitated and their heads placed on pikes along the river levee to warn against further transgression. Charles Delondes himself faced a harsher still punishment. His hands were cut off, presumably as the instruments of his rebellion. He was then shot in each thigh so that he could not run anymore. Before he expired, having been shot multiple times, he was burned alive in a bundle of straw.[32]

The darkness of January 1811 could hardly be overshadowed. Still, sorrow and human tragedy seemed to cling to the estate like the Spanish moss floating above the lawn. Nicholas Noel Destrehan was born to Jean Noel and Marie Celeste de Logny in 1793.[33] At eighteen years old, he no doubt would remember well the Delondes incident for years to come. Whether it affected his persona or not, he was known as a brilliant man plagued by many sullen moods. In time, he began to experience his own personal tragedies.

In 1814, Nicholas became entranced with a young planter's daughter from a prominent family. They married quickly and appeared to be very happy together. His bride fell ill and died soon thereafter, before they had any children together. Nicholas was grief stricken and visibly sullen. He designed her tomb as a testament to his devotion to her. Nicholas did remarry, but he was buried alongside his first love.[34]

Not long after his wife's untimely death, Nicholas was inspecting a piece of grinding machinery in the plantation's sugar mill when his trademark black cape became caught in the moving parts. His hand and arm were snagged and mangled, and he became stuck. In a moment of clearheaded desperation, he yelled to a nearby slave to chop his arm off in order to save his life. The slave did not move, perhaps paralyzed in fear. Nicholas took up the hatchet himself and lopped off the remainder of his mangled arm to free himself from the machinery. He would live for many years, but with his predominant hand severed, he thereafter signed his official correspondence simply "Destrehan, maimed."[35] Nicholas also lost his youngest daughter and his second wife to yellow fever. He became increasingly withdrawn and sent the remainder of his children away to convents or hired personal tutors to care for them daily. Nicholas, widowed twice and reclusive, died an immensely prosperous yet deeply cynical man.[36]

Portrait of Zelia Destrehan Henderson. *Courtesy of Destrehan Plantation and the River Road Historical Society.*

The next generation to reside at Destrehan was formed through the union of Stephen Henderson and Elinore Zelia Destrehan. Henderson purchased the estate at public auction for the fantastic sum of $186,971, returning the property once more to the family.[37] Henderson was a self-proclaimed self-made Scottish immigrant who claimed to have come to the United States penniless. The historic record of their marriage does not lend itself to a tale of complete marital bliss. She was young, attractive and Catholic. He was much older, mocked by many and a Protestant. Their marriage produced no children, and there is little indication they lived together much, if at all.[38] In 1830, Elinore left Louisiana to live, presumably for a time, in New York. She would not return, dying mysteriously in a New York City hotel at age thirty. Curiously, her younger brother would suffer a remarkably similar fate, dying in a New York hotel at the age of twenty-eight. Each death was the result of an unrecorded cause.[39]

Despite his best efforts, Henderson left little lasting influence on the estate after his death in 1838. His will specified that many (but not all) slaves would be freed upon his death, through a complex and calculated timetable that stretched the course of twenty-five years (with predetermined groups released every five years). Once freed, each individual would be offered $100 for safe passage to Africa, where the freeman colony of Liberia was developing. For the remainder of slaves who were not entirely freed, he desired for the plantation itself to be repurposed into a clothing factory to employ the semi-freemen who wanted to stay in Louisiana or for other poor immigrants.[40] Although his father-in-law outlived him for a time, Nicholas's retreat to another family property around the time of his second wife's death made the will feasible. Henderson was evidently trying to make well by this postmortem gesture. However, it takes little reason to note that with no wife and children tying himself to the family, he had nothing to lose from his request. His earthly fortune had already been acquired dealing and living off of enslaved people. The will was contested by Nicholas's remaining children, and the estate was returned to the family about a year later.[41]

Judge Pierre Adolph Rost acquired Destrehan Plantation from the family estate shortly after Henderson's death. Naturally, in the Louisiana way, Rost appears to have helped the family rid themselves of the terms of the Henderson will in court.[42] Judge Rost had married a widowed Destrehan, Louise Odile, daughter of Jean Noel, in New Orleans some years prior. Judge Rost was a French patriot and no doubt a much more attractive potential patriarch for a family in need of one. As a young man, he had fought for Napoleon Bonaparte in France. After Napoleon's defeat and exile, Rost exiled himself to the former French colony of Louisiana in 1815.[43] He was eventually able to pull the estate out of the doldrums and increase the family fortune enough to fund substantial, and now defining, architectural modifications to the old Creole manor. The judge, reportedly under the close supervision of his bride, began updating the Destrehan big house in the Classical Revival style around 1840, employing chunky Doric columns across the gallery, decorative trim and a close attention to the adherence of symmetry in window and door placement that was not evident in its prototypical Creole form. Inside, previously exposed joists in the ceiling were boxed and plastered in. Doors were replaced with larger and more refined classical examples, and a grand staircase, foyer and covered carriage park for guests were completed.[44]

By the mid-1850s, Destrehan Plantation was the largest producer of sugar cane in the area. Judge Rost's wealth and influence grew through the high period of plantation culture. Finally, aided by a family connection from Mississippi, Rost was appointed by Confederate president Jefferson Davis as the minister to France during the Civil War. His absence and French nationality would help save the estate from wartime destruction. During the war, with the entire family away in France, the Destrehan big house was used by the Union army and Federal government as a Freedmen's Bureau and refugee camp for former slaves, ironically partially fulfilling Stephen Henderson's desires for the estate from a generation prior.[45] For a time (1865–67), the Rost Home Colony, as the government referred to it, taught newly freed slaves citizenship and how to function as a free and independent people. Today, one of the rooms that served as an office for the Freedmen's Bureau is furnished and dedicated for the interpretation of this unique time.[46]

After the war, the Destrehan family would reoccupy the estate until 1914, when the plantation property became the location of an oil refinery constructed by Mexican Oil Company (later American Oil Company, later still Amoco). A company town was also built around the site, with railroads stretching across the once fertile sugar cane fields. Initially, oil company executives would reside in the house. Louisiana folk author Lyle Saxon seems to have found this arrangement somewhat peculiar, along with the appearance of the house he described as "restored beyond recognition" and appearing to be "almost new." Later still, the house was used as a company clubhouse and administrative office. Finally, in 1958, the outdated refinery was dismantled, and the big house stood vacant until the formation of the River Road Historical Society in the late 1960s.[47] It was during this brief but destructive time that it was almost constantly vandalized due to the eternal Jean Lafitte legend. In 1994, Destrehan Plantation achieved further notoriety on the national stage as a prominent filming location for the motion picture production of Anne Rice's *Interview with a Vampire*, a southern gothic film set largely in Creole Louisiana in the early nineteenth century.[48]

Portrait believed to be of the pirate Jean Lafitte. *Courtesy of Rosenberg Library, Galveston, Texas.*

Destrehan Plantation is widely regarded by enthusiasts of the supernatural as a quintessentially haunted place. From the ghost of "pirate" Jean Lafitte to former owners from the past, to children forever dwelling within its walls and locked in infinite youth, there remains little of the traditional specter outlets unutilized. Nonetheless, the house is officially not haunted. At least the party line of the River Road Historical Society says so. This "prohibition on apparitions" served a clear purpose: lose the ghosts and end the vandalism. While some historic sites use ghost stories to draw crowds, at Destrehan, it was long drawing the wrong crowds.[49] Just for good measure, the house has also reportedly been exorcised.[50]

By the 1970s, legends of the plantation house's unearthly inhabitants had become so widespread, coupled perhaps with its absentee landowner (a petroleum company) and quick access from the highway at a short drive from New Orleans, that ghost and treasure seekers had devastated much of the property. Contributing perhaps in largest part to this destruction was the legendary ghost of Jean Lafitte, pointing an eerie finger at the location of his long-buried treasure.[51] Interestingly, Lafitte is believed by some to appear in the historic record as having visited Destrehan Plantation, lending a faint credence to the old folktale.[52]

The story goes that on dark and stormy nights (this is, of course, a spectral prerequisite for apparitions) Lafitte appears on the property, some say within the house, and points at the location of his long-lost treasure—sometimes at a certain fireplace within. What treasure that is might be anyone's guess. Lafitte's most lucrative commodity along the River Road community was probably everyday items, black market wine, luxuries and other household items plantation owners didn't want to pay full price for. Another profitable commodity would be illegally imported slaves. Lafitte and his brother would make a living trading human beings for a time, illegally importing Africans past federal authorities. It is this finger-pointing wraith that caused so much destruction within the house over the years, prompting the River Road Historical Society to take an official position on the matter, declaring the house a "Ghost Free Zone" in 1971.[53]

Beyond Lafitte, "disturbances" throughout the house, footsteps in seemingly empty rooms, unexplained voices, "cold zones" and reports of blinking lights persist through the modern era.[54] Among the more dramatic tales heard along River Road is a Destrehan legend concerning the return of a ghostly relative from around the turn of the century. As the tale goes, a lady comes to call on the family of the house. She awaits her hostess in the parlor when at once she sees an old white-bearded gentleman enter the

Dawn at Destrehan Plantation. *Photograph by Cheryl H. White.*

room and wander almost aimlessly about for a moment, only to leave by the same door he entered and without uttering a word to her. When the visitor mentions the queer incident, the hostess responds in disbelief; the man she is describing was ill in a sanitarium in New Orleans. Soon afterward, word came of the old man's death, which of course corresponded with the time of the strange sighting and contributes the dramatic denouement to the tale.[55]

Destrehan Plantation's big house, an overseer's house and two relocated slave cabins form the interpretive core of the former plantation. There are also Creole-style guest cottages available on the estate. The plantation is open daily, with the exception of major holidays, and is readily accessible from Louisiana Highway 48 on the north bank of the Mississippi River Road. As recently as October 2016, the River Road Historical Society tripled the land composing the historical site. The plantation is arguably the largest tourist attraction in St. Charles Parish, Louisiana. The master plan for the plantation calls for an event rental facility for celebrations, six on-site bed-and-breakfast cottages and additional support buildings. The master plan improvements are scheduled for completion in 2018.[56]

DESTREHAN PLANTATION
13034 River Road
Destrehan, LA 70047
(985) 764-9315

CHAPTER 4

THE ARMS OF CENTURIES

OAK ALLEY PLANTATION

Their scaled gray arms arc high into the air above like a nineteenth-century honor guard holding an arch of sabers aloft. It is here that you dare to pass through, that you dream of sharing a place in time with the glamour of the old ways. They are the live oaks at Oak Alley, and they form an unmistakable spectacle that is an invitation through a fabled entrance, charming and daring at once. Beyond the *allée*, a platoon of massive white columns is dressed in a neat square formation. This cultural landscape is burned in the collective southern memory, regardless of whether the place has actually been seen in person. It is a shared space that connects all Louisianans with the audacious history. This iconic juxtaposition of nature and the built environment symbolizes all that is loved and all that is hated, both man's ability to create with majesty and man's ability to be cruel without impunity. If it is to be a symbol then, a graphical representation of the American South, let it be a bold one.

In this manner, Oak Alley has become the omphalos of all iconic imagery readily summoned when contemplating great plantation locales of the Deep South. Indeed, along the Great Mississippi River Road that stretches from New Orleans to Baton Rouge, near the quaint town of Vacherie, Louisiana, there is perhaps no structure more instantly recognizable for its place in popular culture and within the imagination than the imposing Greek Revival edifice of Oak Alley Plantation. Although its colonnade of huge Doric columns makes for instant architectural appeal, it is the aforementioned double row of massive live oak trees that line the *allée*,

Oak Alley Plantation. *Library of Congress, Prints and Photographs Division, Historic American Buildings Survey.*

approximately eight hundred feet long, from which the home draws its current name.

Amid the deeply lush environs of verdant green oaks, it seems folly to suggest that such a place would not somehow be inhabited by the spirits of a long-past age. In fact, the oak trees predate the house by as much as one hundred years, and the origin and meaning of their symmetrical planting remains as much a mystery as the many ghosts of the past within the home's interior.

Someone planted these twenty-eight trees eighty feet apart, in a nearly perfect row, in an *allée* once leading to the river's edge but today stopping at the River Road. Secondary sources allude to an unknown French colonial settler who may have planted the oaks, but the mystery may never be solved with certainty. Historians believe that riverboat captains may have first dubbed the plantation "Oak Alley" and likely would have used it as a landmark navigation point given its almost-certain high visibility. Today, draped in picturesque Spanish moss, the signature oak trees continue to

The *allée* of oaks, from which Oak Alley derives its name. *Photograph by Cheryl H. White.*

frame the beautiful and legendary plantation home constructed from 1837 to 1839. While it might be the perfect setting for a ghost story or two, it is also a sentinel of colonial and Louisiana history, as well as a landmark within the story of a nation.

American writer Mark Twain might have been writing specifically about Oak Alley when he penned this eloquent description of the Great Mississippi River Road upon a visit there:

> *From Baton Rouge to New Orleans, the great sugar plantations border both sides of the river all the way, and stretch their league-wide levels back to the dim forest-walls of bearded cypress in the rear. Shores lonely no longer. Plenty of dwellings, all the way, on both banks—standing so close together, for long distances, plenty of dwellings, so that the broad river lying between two rows, becomes a sort of spacious street. A most home-like and happy-looking region. And now and then you see a pillared and porticoed great manor house, embowered in trees.*[57]

Long before Louisiana became the property of the United States and was admitted to the federal Union in 1812, French and Spanish settlers were unquestionably cultivating these fertile lands along what is now the fabled River Road. Because changing conditions in Europe wrought political instability in the sugar-producing islands of the Caribbean by the eighteenth century, the rise of south Louisiana as a viable alternative for the much-desired crop seemed a natural occurrence. Within the same historical context, the Louisiana colony passed from French control to the Spanish following the Treaty of Fontainebleau in 1762, and the Spanish government encouraged settlement by generously giving away land grants. Usually, local officials allowed settlers to assume control of lands before such grants were even formally approved and recorded in order to expedite the importation of a Spanish identity to the area.

In fact, the land where Oak Alley sits has a history rooted in a grant made under Spanish rule of Louisiana between 1763 and 1800 and finally became part of the vast holdings of sugar planter Valcour Aime that are recorded in 1820.[58] Valcour Aime, also known as the "Louis XIV of Louisiana," was one of the wealthiest men of the late colonial and early American eras in Louisiana and probably cultivated the Oak Alley lands long before they became associated with the existing plantation identity. Regardless, the story of Oak Alley Plantation as it stands today truly began with Jacques Telesphore Roman, who was Aime's brother-in-law. Roman was born in 1800 in Opelousas, Louisiana, the son of notable Creole parents and the brother of Louisiana governor Andre Roman.

It was Jacques Roman who commissioned George Swainey to build the home he envisioned, to be named *Bon Sejour* (a good or pleasant stay), on the grounds of that already-existing sugar plantation. The Roman family came from Grenoble, France, in the mid-eighteenth century prior to the colony's transfer to Spain, and they were able to build a network of farms and plantations throughout southeastern Louisiana. The resulting wealth is expressed in the design and construction of the home, which features the framing of large exterior wraparound galleries. The twenty-eight surrounding Doric columns might have been an intentional means of mimicking the twenty-eight oaks that line the alley, another play on man's toying with the majesty of nature. There is a central hall on both floors that runs the length of the mansion from front to rear. In addition, the mansion's twelve-foot ceilings, with fully operable windows and doors to create cross-currents from opposing galleries, created a respite from the notorious Louisiana summer heat. More than a few histories have correctly observed that while the large and picturesque houses were the most compelling feature of the Louisiana plantation, they were the least important of the structures, since it was only a dwelling place for the family and had little to do with production or output.[59] In spite of this routinely practical observation about the reality of Louisiana plantation life, the structure that remains at Oak Alley today is one of the most beautiful along the River Road.

The story of the Roman family is both inspiring and tragic. The rise to wealth and political notoriety that the family enjoyed is a testament to the much-hoped-for promise of a life in the New World, where immigrants could pursue dreams unencumbered by the old-world expectations and social class restrictions. However, the Louisiana planter class lifestyle had its own unique social limitations and restrictions, and the subtropical climate brought significant challenges to health and quality of life. Dubbed the "White Plague," the ever-present lung malady of tuberculosis claimed more than a few lives throughout the South, and the Roman family did not escape its curse. The disease claimed patriarch Jacques Roman in April 1848, whereupon the management of the plantation enterprise fell to his wife, Celina, and their son, Henri.

Jacques's death proved to be only the first of the misfortunes to strike the family. Celina had no interest in the plantation after her husband's death, preferring a New Orleans lifestyle reportedly so expensive that it strained the family finances.[60] A daughter, Marie, died in 1855 at the age of eleven. Another daughter, Louise, developed gangrene from a freak accident involving a metal wire from her hoopskirt, resulting in the loss of her leg. While there are many stories that widely circulate about the immediate precipitating cause of Louise's accident, historians may never fully know the details. Whether it was a simple fall on the stairs or whether Louise was fleeing the advances of an overly aggressive suitor, the end result was the same. Upon recovering from the illness and ensuing amputation, Louise Roman left Bon Sejour and entered a Carmelite order in St. Louis before moving to New Orleans as mother superior of a new convent established there in 1877.[61]

Like many of the planter families of the antebellum era, the Romans lost their personal fortunes by the end of the Civil War. Although the plantation suffered no structural damages as a result of the conflict, the economic disruptions of war nevertheless posed significant challenges. The interruption of sugar production and wartime impediments to trade sealed the fate of many of the old antebellum plantations. In 1866, Bon

The long and expansive front galleries at Oak Alley Plantation. *Library of Congress, Prints and Photographs Division, Historic American Buildings Survey.*

Sejour was sold at auction for a fraction of its prewar value, purchased by John Armstrong. Jacques and Celina's daughter Octavia Roman, by then married to Philip Buchanan of New Orleans, remained actively involved in helping to administer the plantation after its sale,[62] although Octavia died in 1867.

A former Confederate veteran named Antonio Sobral purchased Oak Alley in 1881 and was able to begin to restore it to some of its prior commercial sugar success. In the early twentieth century, the Hardin family acquired the home and was able to successfully save some of the oak trees from a threatened maneuver of the United States Army Corps of Engineers involving levee works.[63] The march of time and transitions in the Louisiana economy took its toll on many of the antebellum homes along the River Road, and Oak Alley fell into disrepair. This was the story for many of the surrounding plantations, due partly to the spread of Mosaic disease that severely damaged the Louisiana sugar industry. Many of the other plantations in the region would not be saved and are lost except for the pages of history that record where they once stood.

Furthermore, the ongoing economic expansion of the United States and advances in navigation brought unforeseen challenges to the region. The need of dredging the Mississippi River bottom to accommodate large seagoing vessels changed the environment of River Road to an increasingly industrial look and purpose, and the aesthetics of existing structures took on less and less significance over time. Because of the ensuing economic downturn in the sugar industry, coupled with the changing character of the Mississippi River, the transition from the nineteenth to the twentieth century proved to be an era when large numbers of historic structures were lost forever.[64] Fortunately for Oak Alley, the home was purchased in 1925 by Andrew and Josephine Stewart, and architect Richard Koch of New Orleans completed an extensive restoration that preserved its remarkable historical integrity.

Oak Alley is an example of a structure that benefited from a growing awareness of the need for rigorous historic preservation in the early twentieth century. Richard Koch is actually best known for his work with the Historic American Buildings Survey, the first-ever federal preservation program, established during the Depression era. He took charge of the emerging effort in the Greater New Orleans area and was responsible for significant projects such as the one undertaken at Oak Alley and also Shadows-on-the-Teche. The significance of the timing of such awareness of the need for organized preservation efforts cannot be understated. In the photographic documentation of Oak Alley that Koch completed for that project, the perilous state of that plantation in the early twentieth century is obvious.[65] Most importantly, shortly before her death in 1972, Josephine Stewart wisely created a nonprofit organization to manage the property into the future, and today it enjoys the designation of a National Historic Landmark.

A sunlit interior hallway upstairs at Oak Alley. *Photograph licensed by Shutterstock.*

It is actually the restoration of Oak Alley that ushered in a general re-commitment to the great historic structures along the River Road. Fortuitously, in tandem with the historic preservation efforts of the 1920s and beyond, horticultural scientists also worked to develop disease-resistant varieties of sugar cane that brought about a resurgence in that industry across Louisiana, including the River Road region.[66] World War II and its resulting effects on the availability of labor dealt another blow to the industry, due to a lack of manpower available to properly weed and maintain the sugar cane fields. Again, horticultural science met the challenge by providing improved herbicides by the decade of the 1950s.[67] By the mid-twentieth century, just at a time when many sugar farmers in Louisiana were beginning to explore alternative crops or conversion of lands to pasture, these significant developments meant the saving of a centuries-old enterprise. Sugar cane farming was born anew in Louisiana, and with perfect timing for preservationists.

Across south Louisiana, evidence of the commitment to the sugar industry is readily apparent today. However, the overall economic engine of Louisiana's agriculture has successfully driven far more than crop production, with many other tangible benefits that impact virtually every aspect of the surrounding Louisiana economic infrastructure. An economic renewal naturally fueled major historic preservation efforts with fresh interest and new capital, and the result today is that some of these impressive antebellum structures were saved from what otherwise would have been almost certain destruction in the twentieth century.

Today, Oak Alley stands as a popular tourist destination, as well as a frequently sought-after location for movies (*The Long, Hot Summer* and *Interview with the Vampire*), as well as a scenic venue for weddings and special events. The current owners have continued the ongoing maintenance and restoration of the now 180-year-old mansion. In addition, they have begun a noteworthy permanent exhibition to honor the lives of the slaves who lived on the grounds during the antebellum period.

Furthermore, a comprehensive slave database project is underway that documents the known names of those who lived and died in the service of the sugar plantation. The database makes available to the public all information that is presently verified about the Oak Alley slave population. With records drawn together mostly from extant sources such as the St. James Parish Courthouse, the Archdiocese of Baton Rouge and archival records at Tulane University, the database project highlights a tragic reality of plantation life in Louisiana—that the slave population represents a mostly undocumented aspect of its history. This is not a condition unique to Oak Alley but one that challenges many other such historic plantations as well. Reconstructed slave cabins tell the story of life much different than that of the stately "big house." The small cabins, called "doubles," were cramped spaces shared by two families, and living conditions were harsh. Unfortunately, with so little historical documentation available, the efforts to fully tell this aspect of plantation history often prove frustrating.

One of the most interesting aspects of the scantly documented slave history at Oak Alley involves a gardener known simply as Antoine, who in 1846 was credited as being the first to successfully graft pecan trees. It was Antoine who created the first variety of pecan tree to ever be named (the "Paper Shell"), and this achievement has secured his place in horticultural history.[68] There can be no question that the great plantation of the past, today limited to its twenty-five-acre environs, continues to draw heavily upon and simultaneously promote its historical legacy.

There is also a popular draw to the location due to the numerous ghost stories that pervade the history of Oak Alley. All uniquely cemented in the actual historical narrative, the haunted tales from the plantation all serve to underscore the very real lives of those who once called it home. Whether the ghost stories involve the patriarch and founder of Oak Alley, Jacques Roman, or its twentieth-century preservationist Josephine Stewart, the lore derives from the site's documented history. Interviews with the plantation staff revealed a variety of commonly repeated stories from both visitors and workers.

One of the most commonly heard stories involves the occasional overwhelming scent of roses within the Lavender Room, believed to be a reminder of the life of Josephine Stewart, who loved roses and cultivated them on the grounds. All the bedrooms are located on the mansion's second floor, and the Lavender Room is purported to be the one where Josephine Stewart spent her last years. Workers also claim to have seen a man believed to be the original owner, Jacques Roman, on numerous occasions, walking around the mansion's galleries and occasionally peeking inside. Visitors have also reported seeing the ghostly figure of a distinguished man in nineteenth-century formal wear, even in broad daylight, before mysteriously vanishing from view. In a more demonstrative example of a paranormal encounter, one worker related that silverware has been known to fly off the main dining room table, along with candlesticks and other objects. On the exterior galleries, rocking chairs mysteriously move with no one visible. Yet these are the stories that one might expect from a place richly steeped in romance, family drama and tragedy.

The imprint of the past on the structure today is tangibly manifested in the promotion of its haunted folklore and also intersects with the cause of historic preservation. The paranormal aspect appeals to the imagination of those who might not otherwise be drawn by the exemplary architecture or colonial and antebellum historical narrative. Those who visit Oak Alley seeking the ghost of Jacques Roman will inevitably encounter the documented story of his family and their place within the broader framework of Louisiana history. Those who come in curiosity, seeking the aroma of roses in the mansion's fabled Lavender Room, will certainly learn of one woman's noble efforts to save a significant historic structure from sure deterioration and loss. Anyone strolling the grounds hoping to encounter ghostly apparitions in broad daylight will come face to face with the harshest reality of the antebellum plantation economy—that of human slavery.

In this way, the paranormal allure only reinforces the history lesson, and all who visit will go away with a deeper knowledge and bearing the indelible imprint of the past. Long ago, this quarter-mile *allée* of oaks marked a pathway to the edge of the mighty Mississippi River, the central economic hub of a growing and prosperous nation. Oak Alley Plantation, for all its picturesque surrounds, stands simultaneously apart yet fully within the story of a colony, its immigrants and a nation one day ravaged by civil war. Its significance is surely not lost in a ghost story or two.

Oak Alley Plantation
3645 Highway 18
Vacherie, LA 70090
(225) 265-2151

CHAPTER 5

WHITE CASTLES AND BLACK LABOR

NOTTOWAY PLANTATION

M arcus Aurelius once wrote, "Time is a sort of river of passing events, and strong is its current; no sooner is a thing brought to sight than it is swept by and another takes its place, and this too will be swept away." One need only take the gently winding drive down the Great River Road to see the metaphor of time as a river and yet find that the inverse is also true. The river is also like time, and the changes wrought by both are obvious here. The ravages of time have erased many of the magnificent homes that once stood overlooking the Mississippi River, and meanwhile, the river has done what all rivers do—it has changed its course and played no small part in altering the land and its structures. Man can do little except find humility in the work of time and the river, as both move eternally outside his control.

The drive along River Road features a predictably verdant green landscape on the inland side, punctuated by both modern structures and antebellum homes such as those explored elsewhere in this text. There stands an impressive levee on the river side, reflecting the vision of modern engineering to control the volatile elements that come with proximity to such a major waterway as the Mississippi. Nowhere along this storied drive between the cities of Baton Rouge and New Orleans can be found a more stunning edifice than Nottoway Plantation near the small community known as White Castle, Louisiana. The name is perhaps no accident. Although once nearby was a plantation known as White Castle, the name is also quite descriptive of one man's dream to build the greatest home that Louisiana would ever see.

Oblique view of Nottoway Plantation. *Photograph by Cheryl H. White.*

Some three decades before George Washington Vanderbilt II completed construction on the iconic American castle known as the Biltmore Estate in North Carolina, there was construction of a smaller-scale castle underway along frontage of the Mississippi River undertaken by John Hampden Randolph. Of course not equal to Biltmore in scale, Nottoway nevertheless represents a similar spirit in its design planning and construction. Biltmore's opulence can be explained by the extravagant wealth of the Gilded Age in America near the turn of the twentieth century, but the grandeur and scale of Nottoway Plantation belongs to another equally ambitious time. Still considered the largest antebellum plantation house in the South, Nottoway boasts fifty-three thousand square feet of native cypress construction, accented by priceless Italianate marble and crystal chandeliers, framed in classical Greek style. With only sixty-four rooms compared to Biltmore's three hundred, the scale of Nottoway's imprint on the River Road landscape still provokes a similar response from the human senses. At first sight, it is overwhelming, towering above the surrounding cane fields and stretching out in seemingly endless directions. It is indeed Louisiana's version of an American castle, and it gleams white in the sunlight.

In the darkness, the white façades of the mansion today are illuminated with electric lights unknown to its original designer, even as innovative as he was. Also in the darkness is found another aspect of Nottoway's history, for many witnesses insist that there are ghosts that still roam the seemingly endless halls and rooms of the house. Because one might see the specter of its first owner or a more recent one of the late twentieth century, Nottoway's appeal to the visitor extends beyond its architectural charm and its significant place in history. Of course, the haunted lore only contributes to its romantic allure.

Like many of the great mansions of the antebellum era in Louisiana, Nottoway is privileged to still exist. Those homes that survived the Civil War did so because of courage, scheming or sheer luck—and perhaps often a combination of all three. In the case of Nottoway, its survival is due to fortuitous events that occurred both during the war and after. Randolph's wife, Emily, remained on the estate throughout the war, while John Randolph leased land to farm in Texas. An often-repeated tale explains that Nottoway was spared because the commander of a Union gunboat positioned on the river ordered that firing upon the structure must cease. This unverifiable tale holds that this particular commander had once stayed at Nottoway and was impressed by its beauty and architectural dignity. As if to underscore the certitude of the saga, a small cannonball can still be found wedged within an upstairs wall. The survival of the plantation into the post-Reconstruction

The Randolph family graveyard at Nottoway Plantation. *Photograph by Robin Castaldi, courtesy of Nottoway Plantation.*

period is mostly a testament of cunning and determined persuasion on the part of John Hampden Randolph, who was one of many prominent southerners who simply purchased a pardon from President Andrew Johnson in 1867. This turned out to be an act that ensured he would retain ownership of his beloved estate.[69]

The sheer size and wealth of the sugar industry dominated the entire history of this part of Louisiana in the eighteenth and nineteenth centuries, and Nottoway Plantation is no exception. John Hampden Randolph made a fortune in the sugar cane business, and his wealth inspired him to build a showplace on the Mississippi River that would have no rival. Randolph came from a long lineage of the planter aristocracy of Nottoway County, Virginia, from a family with ties to Thomas Jefferson. Born in 1813 in the midst of the early American republic's conflict with Great Britain, his love of his Virginia roots is obviously what inspired the naming of the plantation home he was destined to build one day in Louisiana. In 1819, when John was just six years old, his father was appointed by President James Monroe as a federal circuit court judge in the newly created state of Mississippi. The Randolph family moved south and took up cotton farming at Elmwood Plantation, where John grew into adolescence and met and married Emily Liddell in 1837.[70] The couple eventually had ten children together.

By 1841, like so many other farmers throughout the Deep South, John Randolph turned his interest and energy to the idea of sugar cane cultivation and made the decision to move to neighboring Louisiana. The family's first home was actually Forest Home Plantation, another cotton-producing interest, and the Randolphs would have to wait over a decade to realize the dream of owning vast sugar cane fields and an American castle on the banks of the Mississippi River. In 1844, John borrowed enough money to build a steam-powered mill for sugar cane processing, as well as a levee and drainage system. By this time, he was fully committed, and the conversion from cotton to sugar cane was fully underway.

In the interim, yellow fever made a catastrophic visit to Louisiana in 1853, and on scale, it was the worst epidemic of the disease to ever hit the state. Claiming over eight thousand victims, the mosquito-borne virus ravaged nearby New Orleans. This was also a time when Louisiana's sugar crop was producing rich returns. Unfortunately, by the time of fall harvest, much of that crop likely still sat in New Orleans on unattended docks in an international port city paralyzed by a federal quarantine in effect. Many of the plantations along the River Road were doubtlessly affected by economic circumstances beyond their control, and this may at least partially explain

A portrait of the Randolph family that hangs at Nottoway Plantation. *Courtesy of Nottoway Plantation.*

the sudden availability of land for purchase. Whereas Randolph had been previously unsuccessful in expansion efforts, by 1855, his patience had clearly begun to pay off.

The following year, Emily Liddell Randolph inherited her father's estate, and this contributed to the couple's growing wealth and ability to expand operations.[71] John Randolph began purchasing small tracts of land as they became available, and soon enough, he had acquired all the land near where Nottoway Plantation stands today, with his final holding reaching just over seven thousand acres.[72] In fact, he continued to expand in the years immediately following the Civil War, at a time when others were losing their properties. In 1871, Randolph acquired Bayou Goula plantation at auction because its prewar owner was bankrupted.[73]

John Randolph insisted that he would spare no expense in the construction of his dream home that would face the Mississippi River, and he hired noted New Orleans architect Henry Howard to carry out the formidable task. The Irish-born Howard made a name for himself in the city's Garden District, where he distinguished himself by making generous

The White Ballroom at Nottoway Plantation, with its stunning and exquisite detail.
Photograph by Robin Castaldi, courtesy of Nottoway Plantation.

use of classical elements in his designs.[74] Construction began in 1857 and was fully completed by 1859. John Randolph had his wish: the finished home was indeed like nothing Louisiana had ever seen before. Throughout the house, the architect included the finishing touch of exquisite frieze plaster work, with elaborate cornice designs and hand-carved molding, beautifully preserved to this day. The imposing three-story structure was successfully raised from the dirt of cane fields as a visible symbol of Randolph's success, as well as (perhaps) his vanity. Reportedly, Randolph destroyed the architectural plans for Nottoway once the project was completed to prevent anyone from attempting to imitate it.[75]

The mansion featured several innovations that were quite unexpected for its day, including three bathrooms with running water and flushing toilets made possible by the addition of cisterns in the attic that collected rainwater and distributed it through a pipe system. There was gas lighting throughout the house, thanks to Randolph's installation of his own gas plant on the property. In addition to its distinction in decoration and innovation, the house featured the fun practicality of a bowling alley for the Randolph children.[76] The gardens of the home were the final feature to be completed and originally included the plantings of live oaks, which are a signature of the Great River Road. However, much of the frontage of the house was eventually altered by the changing course of the river, as well as additional levee work in the mid-twentieth century. Today's landscape bears little resemblance to the vast views that the Randolphs would have enjoyed from their galleries. Certainly, the description provided by Cornelia Randolph Murrell of the frontal impression of her childhood home is no longer true:

> *Across the public road from the foot of the levee, a stately gate with a small one on either side for pedestrians, guarded the carriage approach which wound at leisure over the front pasture through groups of catalpa, magnolia, and other trees, until it reached a green iron carriage gate dividing a low hawthorn hedge....When the drive left the poplars it turned around a circle leading to the mansion and through which a narrow walk rambled.*

The Randolphs owned Nottoway until 1889. Fortunately, unlike many other plantation homes of the Deep South, there has never been a time in the structure's history when it has been vacant or abandoned. This turn of fortune has meant that even though the Mississippi River has wrought significant change to the land, the "castle" of the Randolph family has enjoyed ongoing efforts at preservation and loving care. Today, Nottoway Plantation attracts visitors from all over the world, drawn not just to the historic home itself but also to its gardens and recently added resort accommodations. It has embraced the modern era in a way that preserves its historical integrity yet acknowledges twenty-first-century technologies and comforts.

Yet, as with all these antebellum plantations, there is another side to the history of Nottoway, one that cannot be ignored. This plantation was the result of wealth built upon the labor of human slaves, who worked under grueling conditions to harvest a crop that was notoriously fickle in the unpredictable Louisiana subtropical climate. There can be no question that conditions for these individuals must have been beyond our ability to truly appreciate or comprehend.

Although the figures likely do not reflect the peak of his slaveholdings, the 1860 United States census shows that at the time, Randolph owned 155 slaves and the Nottoway grounds included forty-two slave cabins (known as "the quarters"), as well as a meetinghouse and hospital for the slaves.[77] It is part of the rich oral tradition of the plantation that at least one slave, named Judah, escaped and was able to join the Union army.[78] Interestingly,

Randolph contracted with over 50 of his former slaves to remain on and work at Nottoway following their emancipation.[79]

One of the most poignant stories in the lore of Nottoway Plantation involves a married slave couple, Nicodemus and Elizabeth Flowers, whom Randolph acquired at the New Orleans slave market. Randolph initially rejected the pair because he wanted only to acquire Nicodemus and had a rule of not separating families. However, a family diary relates that Elizabeth begged Randolph to purchase them both, since she feared the next buyer would not be so merciful. Randolph relented and brought the pair to Nottoway.

Nicodemus drowned in an accident on the river before the Civil War, but Elizabeth stayed with the Randolph family until her death and is one of the former slaves to remain in Randolph's employ following emancipation. That relationship continued for generations. The history of the Randolph family shows that Nicodemus and Elizabeth Flowers's granddaughter was married in the main dining room at Nottoway.[80]

Three of the Randolph sons went to war on behalf of the Confederacy, and one of them, Algernon Sidney Randolph, was killed during the Siege of Vicksburg in 1863.[81] Oral tradition also holds that another son was disinherited because he fled Nottoway with a female slave.[82] This was a time in history that produced many such dramatic events, and the inevitable imprint of history upon a place engenders a folklore that is unique to its conditions, environs and personalities. Nottoway still has the unmistakable echoes of its past resonating in a rich supernatural allure all its own.

The plantation purportedly features a variety of ghostly tales, enough to satisfy anyone with a paranormal curiosity. The popular legend is that Nottoway's original owner, John Hampden Randolph, still roams the halls of his massive home, and why wouldn't he? The family plot where he rests is on the side lawn, and the palatial home and grounds certainly represent his life's work. In 2009, Nottoway was featured in an episode of the Discovery Channel's *GhostLab* series, and the investigative team from the network had some interesting and unusual findings. Among their findings were a sighting of Randolph's apparition, unexplained voices within the house and the simultaneous movement of objects from one location to another. One of the team's investigators captured a photographic image of a woman's face reflected in a third-floor window overlooking the Mississippi River.[83] Their findings seem to support what visitors and workers at Nottoway Plantation have long reported: quite simply, the house is haunted by those who lived and worked there before.

Nottoway Plantation, front elevation, view from the Great River Road. *Photograph by Cheryl H. White.*

John Randolph died in September 1883 and is buried in the family plot at Nottoway. He left his entire estate to his wife, Emily, although by the time of his death, Randolph had sold off all but approximately eight hundred acres and the main house at Nottoway. Emily Jane Randolph sold the plantation in 1889 and divided the proceeds of $50,000 among the couple's surviving children.[84]

The home has been through a succession of owners in the twentieth century and today is a popular tourist destination. One can stand on the front gallery of Nottoway today and see the mighty Mississippi River in the distance and, perhaps only momentarily, pause to understand Randolph's passion and drive to build his American castle there. For anyone viewing Nottoway from the vantage point of a boat or barge on the Mississippi River, it comes into view with the same stunning grandeur of nearly 160 years ago, and then just as quickly, it is gone from sight.

Time and the river. Both still have much to say about Nottoway Plantation.

NOTTOWAY PLANTATION
30970 Highway 405 (River Road)
White Castle, LA 70788
(225) 545-2730

ONE DUEL, MANY DEATHS

CHEROKEE PLANTATION

Anyone who visits with the idea of encountering the past on the grounds of Cherokee Plantation in Natchez, Louisiana, today will come face to face with a fascinating social reality of life in early America, perhaps especially in the Deep South. Cherokee Plantation is blood-soaked ground, stained by an event from its earliest history that produced the most likely explanation for any paranormal appeal it has today. Like all the sites examined herein, Cherokee has its own unique position in the annals of antebellum Louisiana, and like other plantations of the period, it makes for an interesting architectural study as well as offering its own historical testimony.

There are few surviving examples of Creole architecture outside the state of Louisiana, and of those within the state of Louisiana existing today, there are few that are more representative of French building aesthetics than this home. Built in the signature Creole style, Cherokee embraces many of the characteristic design elements, including a square design, large galleries, unique roofline and, of course, its height from the ground, which is far more imposing than it seems at casual glance. A white picket fence perfectly frames the structure against the contrasts of grass and sky. Just southeast of the historic town of Natchitoches, and sitting on the west bank of the Cane River, Cherokee Plantation falls today within the Cane River National Heritage Area.

Observers have accurately noted that Creole houses in Louisiana seem to float atop the earth, as if held aloft by the sheer force of history. Perhaps nowhere can such a statement be made with more certainty than here, where down a long grassy lane there stands this structural witness to both the inevitable passing of the years and the tragic passing of human life. Firmly placed atop cypress beams that position it six feet off the ground, it is indeed true that this particular structure seems to equally own the earth beneath it and the air above it, as if silently hovering between two worlds: that of the living and of the dead. Cherokee Plantation, the site of a notorious and deadly duel, has seen much in its history and revealed some of its past but has no doubt kept a few secrets as well. Such provocative human drama only adds to its mysterious beauty. Although it is no great mansion by the standards of the opulent sugar palaces along the Great River Road of south Louisiana, this humble and unimposing home is yet a noble reminder of Louisiana's antebellum history and its unique Creole culture and heritage.

To trace the history of Cherokee Plantation requires beginning in 1837, two years before the home was built. That was the year that saw the marriage of Charles Emile Sompayrac to Marie Clarisse Prudhomme. In

The *allée* of oaks at Cherokee Plantation, Natchez, Louisiana. *Photograph by W. Ryan Smith.*

One of the majestic live oaks on the property of Cherokee Plantation covered in resurrection fern. *Photograph by W. Ryan Smith.*

1839, Sompayrac acquired approximately 1,100 acres from his father-in-law, Narcisse Prudhomme, and the construction of Cherokee began. Sompayrac apparently brought a bit of old-world flair to his new environs, and he was noted by contemporaries to have a somewhat bold and brash lifestyle.[85] It is perhaps that aspect of his personality that brought death to his back door, in the form of a duel in the autumn of 1839. In this way, Cherokee Plantation entered the history of the antebellum era in a way completely consistent with and reflective of the social expectations of the time.

Dueling had a code of conduct all its own, governed by rules of honor that date to European ordeals as a way of settling conflicts, particularly personal ones. Although quite common among both English and Creole settlers in the New World, by the time the duel occurred on the grounds of Cherokee Plantation, it was a practice that had been illegal in the United States for nearly forty years. As a matter of fact, dueling was already illegal when Louisiana entered the federal Union in 1812. Yet, as seen many times throughout the history of the early American republic, the law was no impediment to men seeking this type of permanent conflict

Cherokee Plantation, oblique view. Built in the Creole style, the house sits at an elevation of six feet. *Photograph by W. Ryan Smith.*

resolution. It was a time-honored method of restorative justice that would have especially appealed to a Creole population with recent ties to Europe. Such was the case between Francois Gaennie, an adjutant general of the Louisiana militia as well as a politician affiliated with the briefly lived Whig Party, and General Pierre Bossier (also of the Louisiana militia), who was a Democratic congressman.

Pierre Bossier, for whom Bossier Parish in Louisiana is named, was a successful cotton and sugar planter with lands along both the Cane and Red Rivers, and he served in the Louisiana state senate before being elected to Congress.[86] The men had been involved in a political disagreement weeks before at a social gathering, and each claimed insult and injury to their personal integrity. It was Gaennie who issued the duel challenge, to which Bossier did not readily agree. However, Bossier's reticence carried with it the perilous undertone of cowardice, so rather than be denounced publicly in such a way, Bossier reluctantly accepted the challenge.[87]

This interesting code of honor that was at work for Gaennie and Bossier was known across the antebellum South. Perhaps indicative of the rigid class structure that many historians believe characterized both the era and the geographic environment, dueling certainly was a way of asserting a type of superiority over the law. It also made a statement about one's independence from the strict legal accountability that would have applied to common folk. To be clear, this type of formal dueling, which adhered to standard principles of conduct and rules of engagement, was uniquely seen only in areas of developed civilization with a European transplanted population. This was not the kind of "shootout" that characterized the American western frontier, where men from all walks of life tended to ignore rules and conventions that had been historically applied to the honorable art of the duel.[88] This formal dueling witnessed by the antebellum South was deeply rooted in the concept of proper justice among gentlemen and, therefore, was inextricably linked to one's social class. In fact, so pervasive was the practice of the duel among the aristocracy that it seems to have taken the social chaos wrought by the Civil War to finally bring it to an end.

It is perhaps predictable that the American South before the Civil War would be a place rife with potentially explosive political disagreements, and certainly, political insults of one form or another have been the cause of many famous duels. Southerners seem to have particularly engaged in behaviors that implied a personal ownership of political positions, perhaps a trait that can again be ascribed to European aristocratic influences. Private disagreements notwithstanding, to insult one's political position in a public manner was to insult the person himself. Such insults demanded not only an accounting but an act that would restore a measure and balance of honor.

Although it is difficult to make a scholarly estimate about the number of such duels that took place in the Old South, there is good evidence that they were quite frequent in the pre–Civil War era. There are numerous newspaper reports that have survived to indicate the popularity of such deadly encounters, and even those primary sources probably provide an incomplete narrative, since many such events were not reported in the news.[89] Interestingly, however, it was also not unusual for a planned duel, although illegal, to be publicized in the same news outlets in advance.

Although New Orleans enjoyed the reputation of being home to the most recorded face-to-face duels in Louisiana history, Natchitoches Parish certainly saw more than its fair share. This would be an expected statistic, given the history of the settlement and its heavily Creole population. Favorite dueling spots in Natchitoches tended to be at picturesque spots along the Cane River or on the shores of Lake Sibley.[90] The Gaennie-Bossier duel took place right on the Cane River at Cherokee Plantation, presumably chosen for both its privacy and because it was the land of its noted Creole owner. What happened on the morning of September 18, 1839, is the source of some of the most persistent and haunting folklore of the plantation's history.

In a few moments' time that morning, just past 9:00 a.m., one of these men died for the sake of personal honor. It was a fate for which both of them were prepared. Forty paces apart, per the written agreement settled in advance, the men stood facing down a life-or-death decision with rifles in hand. In this case, the final decision was made by Bossier's bullet, which struck Gaennie in the chest and mortally wounded him.[91]

In an account that seems to forebode of Gaennie's death that September morning, he reportedly instructed his wife that should he survive the duel, the news of his success would be delivered to her by a messenger mounted on a white horse. If he were to die, however, the news would be carried by a messenger on a black horse. The distinction seems to be obvious: he intended for his wife to be able to discern the news long before the messenger reached her, abbreviating her period of anxiety if only by the briefest of time.[92]

Unfortunately for Natchitoches Parish, the duel at Cherokee Plantation between Gaennie and Bossier did not result in only one death. Because of the furor over Gaennie's death, the political divisions only intensified, and over the course of the next two years, eleven more men died in violent acts that can be directly traced to that September morning of 1839 on the banks of the Cane River.[93] Death exacts a price, but it is not always claimed in a single payment. While there was only one duel on the grounds of Cherokee, and one ghost left to roam the plantation today, its effect was to bring the deaths of many more. This painful historical truth can be added to the legacy of Cherokee.

Perhaps the final tragic footnote to this story is the ending of Bossier's life. In 1844, while yet a United States congressman for the newly created Fourth District of Louisiana, Bossier took his own life.[94] The personal turmoil that led him to suicide is unknown, but clearly his own death cannot fully be separated from the defining event of Cherokee Plantation just five years previously.

Natchitoches Parish was not spared the visit of further deadly conflict with the arrival of the Civil War. The Union army, which had previously occupied both New Orleans and Baton Rouge, moved northward in the spring of 1864 toward Shreveport. There is no way of knowing the final human toll, direct and indirect, that was caused by the arrival of arms in Natchitoches Parish or how much the lands of Cherokee Plantation might

Above: Front view of Cherokee Plantation. *Library of Congress, Prints and Photographs Division, Historic American Buildings Survey.*

Right: Main gate of Cherokee Plantation in the early twentieth century. *Library of Congress, Prints and Photographs Division, Historic American Buildings Survey.*

have factored in the conflict. Unquestionably, lives of people in the area were disrupted, at a minimum. War wreaks havoc on lives, economies and, sometimes, structures. Cherokee Plantation survived, as did its owners.

Not only did Emile Sompayrac live to see the conclusion of the Civil War, but it is almost poetic that he witnessed the scale of armed conflict waged in the same divisive spirit of the politics at the core of the Gaennie-Bossier duel in 1839. He died in 1878, and his wife, Clarissa, continued to operate the plantation until 1891, although she seems to have been forced to gradually sell off parcels of land that composed the once-vast estate. The first sale took place in 1886, to her attorney, William Jack, who in turn sold the property to Thomas Creighton. It was Creighton who sold the estate to Thomas Murphy in 1891, since which time it has remained among their descendants.[95] Cherokee continued to operate for many more years as a working plantation, and some of its original lands continue to be farmed today.

There is no question that Cherokee Plantation is a place that, because of its history, has perpetuated its own folklore but has also slowly entered popular culture. Folklore is primarily transmitted by personal experience and the intimate transmission of oral stories and popular culture by a wider variety of media. Cherokee can today claim to be part of both traditions of sharing in the great human story.

The visitor to Cherokee Plantation is best warned in advance of the location's dark history and the trail of blood that begins with the untimely death of General Gaennie on its grounds. Although the long-ago duel produced but one violent death on its grounds, it is an event that triggered the shedding of much more blood, and in that way, there could be many ghosts there. When the popular film version of *Steel Magnolias* was being filmed in Natchitoches, actress Shirley Maclaine reportedly visited Cherokee for a tour and had a paranormal encounter in the stairwell leading to the upstairs half story, claiming that she experienced the presence of the ghost of a young man named Charles. This supports a long-standing family story that there was a young man named Charles or Charlie who died on the property in the late nineteenth century after falling from a tree limb and breaking his neck. Among the many tales of Cherokee hauntings, this remains the one that is most often repeated. Across the twentieth century, visitors and guests at Cherokee have reported a variety of eerie experiences, including cold spots in rooms and even one report of a full apparition of a young man standing in one of Cherokee's bedrooms.[96]

A view toward the main house at Cherokee Plantation. *Library of Congress, Prints and Photographs Division, Historic American Buildings Survey.*

Photograph of Cherokee Plantation at the time of the Historic American Buildings Survey Project, circa 1933. *Library of Congress, Prints and Photographs Division.*

The stairway at Cherokee Plantation where paranormal activity has been reported. *Photograph by W. Ryan Smith.*

Today, atop its tall and proud beams, this great old house has unquestionably been a silent witness to life, love, laughter, joy and tragedy. Its affiliation with the history of a violent duel has left a significant lesson behind—that of the ill that humanity can do in the name of honor and just cause. Places associated with sudden and violent death are notoriously cited as ideal locales to encounter ghosts of the past, and if this is true, then Cherokee Plantation cannot possibly disappoint.

Cherokee Plantation
Highway 494
Natchez, LA

CHAPTER 7

THROUGH SWORD AND CINDER

MAGNOLIA PLANTATION

During the time of year when the foliage on the hardwood is at its thickest, when the underbrush and creeping vines curl their way up the trunks of the scrub growth and twist sinuously around the majestic live oaks, the big house at Magnolia Plantation is hardly visible from Louisiana Highway 119. These days, the family would likely tell you they like it that way. Before the house, a rural highway in Natchitoches Parish follows the twisting banks of the Cane River. It is a blacktopped ancient path, and many stately homes can be accessed or at least viewed at a glance from the comfort of an automobile passing along the historic state route. At Magnolia Plantation, the U.S. National Park Service oversees a variety of rare, surviving outbuildings clustered in neat linear patterns across the old estate. This ensemble of plantation structures includes several brick slave cabins, a former slave hospital and an extremely rare mule-driven wooden cotton press—itself an engineering marvel the subject of much documentation by the Historic American Engineering Record. From the vantage point of the National Park Service grounds, through the unbelievable array of rare and intact plantation structures evocative of a former life and time, the big house at Magnolia stands due northwest a mere three hundred feet from the blacktop road. It looms through the surrounding brush, framed by the southern flora like a living impressionist painting. The house calls from beyond the *pigeonnier* and the *bousillage* blacksmith shop. Only the least curious or most lazy among the human race would not naturally want to brave the beckoning thicket for a peek inside to see what lies beyond the neatly bush-hogged park grounds and through the brush. There, beyond the fence line, you may see the stately dormer windows peeking through the clumps of oak leaves floating almost still in the air. A thousand-yard stare from windows? Yes, Magnolia Plantation, were it personified, might be dubbed shy, disenchanted and withdrawn. Yet that cautious outlook comes through experience, immediately recognizable by those who also have suffered. The place bears the scars of war and wears the ravages of time like a silent but knowing veteran at a Memorial Day parade.

The land upon which Magnolia Plantation was established (about twenty miles southeast of Natchitoches, Louisiana) was acquired by Jean Baptiste LeComte I, who came from France to Natchitoches Post sometime between 1750 and 1753, about a decade before the beginning of the Spanish period in the Louisiana colony.[97] By the 1750s, the once remote and sparsely populated frontier outpost of Natchitoches was steadily growing as the local economy began to shift from subsistence farming and frontier living toward planting crops and raising livestock for profitable export downriver to New Orleans and beyond. *Vacheries* (cattle ranches and dairies) were emerging on the east side of the Cane and downriver from the stockade fort. Planters were experimenting with profitable crops, and skilled artisans and merchants were setting up shops to peddle dry goods to relieve the landed class of a measure of their profits.[98] Through years of tropical disease, mismanagement and misfortune, the experiment of the Louisiana colony was at last beginning to pay off—for some.

LeComte (d. 1787) acquired a grant from the colonial government and settled on the land that would become known as Magnolia Plantation in the coming century. Initially, the family appears to have pursued a modest combination of subsistence farming for food and sustenance while tending a small production of tobacco crops for additional income.[99] His son Ambrose LeComte II (b. 1760) served the Spanish government as a cavalryman in the local mounted militia, his name appearing on a muster role dated 1780. The LeComte family farm at this time evidently remained a modest enterprise, comprising fewer than ten cows, some pigs and horses and an annual yield of about two thousand pounds of tobacco on eight *arpents* (about six and three-quarter acres) of land. However, by 1787, the family estate had swelled to sixty-four *arpents* of land and sixty cattle held in the *vacherie*.[100] The family's rise in wealth corresponds closely with the large-scale rise in wealth across the colony.

After the notable success of the Prudhomme family's cotton venture on their land some fifteen miles to the northwest along the River Road, the LeComtes began planting the soon-to-be ubiquitous southern crop in large quantity by the 1830s, acquiring land through a series of what have been described by one historian as "propitious purchases." Around 1835, the LeComte family farm began operating as an almost entirely for-profit plantation. Cattle farming remained, but likely at a reduced importance, perhaps only to provide fresh beef and dairy to the family. Ten years later, the complete LeComte estate was valued at more than $285,000 (more than $7 million in 2015 dollars).[101]

The Magnolia portion, then known simply as LeComte Plantation, contained some 785 acres in 1845, but this was only a fraction of the total land the family owned at that time.[102] Nonetheless, despite his material success, Ambrose LeComte II faced an old European estate paradox: he was without a male heir. As such, a new family name entered the Magnolia Plantation lexicon with the marriage of Atala LeComte to Matthew Hertzog in 1852.[103] By the time the 1860 U.S. Slave Schedule was tabulated, the Magnolia Plantation families were baling more cotton and held more enslaved workers (235) than any other plantation in Natchitoches Parish.[104] The total metamorphosis from remote subsistence farm to family cattle ranch to the prototypical southern antebellum cotton fiefdom was complete.

Yet the LeComte Plantation was physically unlike most in the area. The big house was grand for Natchitoches, whose French customs typically favored a polished utilitarian look over the lavish Greek temple–style homes being built along the Mississippi River. The house was built in the early 1850s and was among the largest in the parish.[105] However, the uniqueness of the place was really found elsewhere. At Magnolia, the quarters—the community where the enslaved workers were housed—was composed of a majority of brick cabins, complete with Greek Revival end return detailing on the side gable houses. Slave families were evidently allowed semi-private spaces, with two families per house (these were likely related family units). A loadbearing and substantial brick wall divided the living spaces through the unusually detailed domestic slave houses. This level of comfort, such as it was in the grip of human slavery, was certainly not universal to the rest of the parish or indeed throughout the South in the period.[106]

Still, enslaved they were, and insurrection and mischievous conduct were part of that existence. During the construction of the big house, a slave named Charles snuck into the unfinished building while the Hertzogs were staying in Natchitoches in their family town house and stole stocks of whiskey, wine and meat (meat itself was a rare luxury for the enslaved).[107] It seems this bout of insubordination was not forgotten, and in time, slave

Slave quarters at Magnolia Plantation, Natchitoches Parish. *Library of Congress, Prints and Photographs Division, Historic American Buildings Survey.*

shackles would appear beneath the porch steps of the big house for the most uncooperative among the plantation hands.

When the idle threats of politicians turned into the flames of war, the LeComte-Hertzog family cast their lot with the Confederacy, and with no half-hearted effort. The family would donate much in treasure and blood to "the cause." This was despite and in face of the prevalent anti-secession sentiment of lower Natchitoches Parish, where the nearby village of Cloutierville voted against secession overwhelmingly and held open "Unionist Club" meetings throughout the war.[108] Nonetheless, the LeComte-Hertzog sacrifice would include slaves sent to aid the Confederate army and a number of their own relatives killed in the tumult.[109] Closer to home, like so many of the grand southern estates, the war would not leave Magnolia Plantation unscathed.

In late March 1864, in the midst of an ominous hailstorm that was recorded throughout diaries of the time, a massive Union army approached Natchitoches Parish from occupied south Louisiana, crossing the Cane River on March 31, just a few miles from Magnolia Plantation. Their route would take them directly past the LeComte-Hertzog estate. The growing number of smoking columns filling the stormy sky with ash foretold the fate that

Elise LeComte and her sister, Cora. *Courtesy of Judge Henley Hunter.*

awaited the remaining downriver residents. Young Elise LeComte recorded in her journal: "The weather is terrible. The Yankees are approaching. We are to be burned. May God have mercy on us."[110]

As fate would have it, the Confederates were the first to torch much of the family fortune. Under orders to burn all valuable cotton and usable accoutrements, lest they be seized by the advancing Union forces, mounted Confederates came to the plantation and burned the gin barn (which was full of baled cotton) and other massive stocks of stored cotton throughout the estate. When the Union army passed the plantation five days later, the fires were still smoldering amid the falling rain, such was the extent of the pyres, the extent of the wealth set ablaze by the riverside.[111]

Bad luck, inept Union leadership and a stiffening resolve from the once-retreating Confederate army brought the Union forces back through the Cane River Valley again in late April 1864, following a disastrous rout at the Battle of Mansfield and a bloody stalemate at the Battle of Pleasant Hill. The angry and humiliated soldiers took out months of frustration and trauma on the residents of the Cane River Valley. Indiscriminate and wanton looting, burning and destruction marked the path of their retreat back to Alexandria. Much of this destruction, held savage in the chronicles of an already grim conflict, has been attributed to soldiers of General A.J. Smith's command both by historians and by eyewitness testimony. Acting as the Union army's rear guard, the soldiers butchered or stole all livestock, burned residences (both slave dwellings and plantation houses alike) and destroyed all vestiges of personal wealth they could find.[112] Were it not for Sherman's march through Georgia, which occurred just a few months later, the destruction would have likely gone down in the annals of war as among the most complete and ruthless.

At the front of the column, the bewildered Union army enlisted the help of a local guide to get them through the area quickly, via shortcuts and backroads to avoid further harassment by the pursuing Rebels. The guide, whose name is lost to history, led them directly to the doorstep of Magnolia Plantation via the River Road toward Cloutierville. At Magnolia Plantation, Confederate cavalry caught up with the Union rear guard and fought a back-and-forth skirmish across the LeComte property throughout the midday of April 22, 1864. Here, the Twenty-First Texas Cavalry fought tired and displaced elements of Union General Lucas's cavalry brigade. Throughout the day and into the next morning, the Confederate cavalry would race headlong into the Union rear guard in one arm of an ambitious and ultimately unsuccessful attempt to bottle up the Union forces on the Isle Brevelle.[113]

Folklore maintains that during the fighting, the big house at Magnolia was empty except for the plantation overseer, a Mr. Miller, and perhaps a domestic servant or two. The family tradition records that Union soldiers approached the house from the short oak *allée* to the River Road and encountered Miller on the porch. To his own peril, he was probably armed. The details of what happened next are unclear, but Miller was shot by the soldiers and died, collapsing on the front steps of the big house. Then the house was set aflame with virtually all its contents. Very little was saved before the inferno burned everything, leaving only the scorched, naked columns, some exterior walls and a pile of smoldering ruin.[114] In just a few hours, the most impressive family estate in Natchitoches Parish was destroyed and its fields were littered with dead and dying men and horses. Following the retreat of the Union army from Cloutierville, Magnolia Plantation would not again see armed conflict on its grounds. The family, which became increasingly known under the Hertzog name in time, moved into the plantation's former slave hospital in what was a supposed temporary necessity. In reality, the Hertzogs would remain in the building for more than thirty years.

Soon after the war, Magnolia Plantation entered the sharecropping and day labor phase of its operation. It was a period that, though seldom studied, would represent by far its longest mode of existence. In the devastated postwar South, Magnolia Plantation became, more than ever before, a community unto its own. While the Hertzog slaves had certainly been freed and no doubt many left the area at their time of liberation, others chose to remain. Out of both necessity and forced political intervention, a new, if uneasy, relationship was formed between the former slaves and their former owners. In the Cane River area, the local commander of occupying Union forces, Lieutenant Colonel S.G. Van Anda, issued orders instructing the freedmen to remain on their former plantations. The freedmen were to negotiate work contracts to get the plantations operational again. Crass though it was, there simply was a need to get the southern economy moving again after the devastating war.[115]

The local Freedmen's Bureau mediated the negotiations with landowners. Nonetheless, there was no doubt malcontent and mistrust between the partners. Mounting issues and hostility toward the contract labor system led many former slaves to refuse to sign or renew their work contracts by 1867. Understandably, the contract system seemed eerily similar to the enslavement from which they had just escaped.[116] In many cases, they were living in the same quarters and working the same fields from their days as slaves.

The sharecropping labor system developed as a more palatable alternative. Eventually followed by poor whites as well as former slaves, sharecropping provided laborers with a possible means of accumulating wealth. The promise of the ability to eventually purchase their own land was alluring. On the other hand, for the landowners and the planter class, the sharecropping system provided a reduced burden of supplying regular cash payments to their laborers—money would be in short supply throughout the

South for generations to come. Further, under the day labor and contract system, the planter would be forced to pay his laborers according to their time put in, regardless of the crop's success or failure. It was assumed that because the sharecropper's fortunes and the landowner's success were now inextricably linked, the system would get the agricultural South back on track economically. All things equal, the system might have worked, but years of hardship remained ahead.[117]

Today, the brick houses of the quarters appear stark and barren, quite uninhabitable. Yet during the sharecropping and day labor era (circa 1867–1960), the houses of the quarters were utilized to their fullest extent for comfort, sustenance and sustainable living. Most of the houses in the quarters had a kitchen added on the backside, to the east toward the cotton fields and the town of Cloutierville. The former slave cabins were also surrounded with vegetable and pepper gardens. Many families raised their own pigs in pigpens. Chickens raced through the yards between the houses and throughout the quarters. Typically, the quarters' residents were paid in wages according to their day's work. These tenants were often non-agricultural laborers and included among their ranks blacksmiths, cooks, stable hands and domestics. Many of the farmhands lived on the periphery, scattered in shotgun houses and cabins near the crops they worked to cultivate.[118]

Once the upheaval of the war and the dramatic societal changes it wrought were absorbed, the Hertzog family resumed its status as the principal agricultural barons of the lower Cane River Valley. As humbling as the war time and postwar rebuilding experiences must have been, a new big house would not be completed until 1897—thirty-three years after Union forces killed the overseer and torched it. The replacement was built right on the same foundation, upon the very piers and utilizing the same columns of their first house, evidently in an almost identical manner. The family was making a statement, it seems, for by the 1890s, a high-style Victorian manor house would have been truer to the fashion of the day. Instead, the house was put back together, almost as if it never left in the first place. The former slave hospital used as the temporary Hertzog residence would in turn become the plantation overseer's house, just in time for the occupation to begin its inevitable fade into history.[119]

On Saturdays, the hub of the Magnolia community (often referred to as "Hertzog's Place" or simply "Mr. Matt's" in later years, in reference to the owner-descendant, Matthew Hertzog) was the plantation store, located within the quarters along the side of the old River Road. In the 1940s, Mr. Matt would make home movies of the song and dance and general southern

View of the Magnolia Plantation big house through the wooded lawn. *Library of Congress, Prints and Photographs Division, Historic American Buildings Survey.*

mirth on these festive days off. The silent footage is a true folk life treasure in a medium that unfortunately cannot be reproduced for these pages but is an absolute pleasure to view. The tenants and the Hertzogs enjoyed watching the films together. The Hertzog store served as the makeshift theater too, where a portable screen was set up by the front door and the lights were extinguished. When the projector was turned on and the reels began to spin, the tenants would delight to see themselves in the films, taunting one another and laughing at themselves. During holidays, especially at Christmas, fiddles and guitars were brought out, and the people danced.[120]

From Magnolia Plantation's earliest days and into the first half of the twentieth century, a horse racing track was maintained on the property. Horse racing was a popular sport throughout Cane River, and there are historical records related to racehorse breeding and inter-plantation rivalries and race matches. At Magnolia, the Hertzogs kept a variety of horses, among them often a number of old and gentle mares that any novice could ride. The Hertzogs would keep ribbons from past horse shows marked first, second or third place, etc., for the quarters residents and sharecropper shows. The events were often fabricated or comical, something that anyone could

Overseer's house, former slave hospital, Magnolia Plantation. *Library of Congress, Prints and Photographs Division, Historic American Buildings Survey.*

participate in safely and to the great amusement of the crowd. Spectacles such as "Ride like a dead man," "The twist on horseback" or simply "Ride backward" were performed with great humor and exaggerated fanfare. The ribbons were always given out by the little girls of the quarters, dressed in their Sunday best.[121]

Despite the congenial celebrations on the weekends, Magnolia Plantation carries a legacy of pain and human suffering that no amount of horse racing, fiddle playing or country recreation has managed to erase. War. Disease. Famine. Slavery. Fires and floods. The drama of the American story played out across the fields and through those quarters. A simple Internet search using any combinations of the words "Magnolia Plantation," "ghost," "haunting," "haunted history" and so on instantly reveals many pages, blogs and personal experience accounts of Magnolia Plantation's growing reputation as a place of many supposed paranormal experiences. The reputation of the site, and perhaps its accessibility, attracted the nationally syndicated television series *Ghost Adventures* to film on location in 2009. The cast went out of their way to conjure ghouls and "disembodied voices" from beyond for the camera.

In the show, the Travel Channel team tempts spirits in the big house and the plantation quarters in one of the former brick slave cabins. The latter, the supposed former home of "legendary healer" Aunt Agnes, who lived well into her hundreds, was the scene of clearly frightened television hosts as they sat opposite each other in antique chairs and tempted Aunt Agnes to communicate with them. For preparation on the evening before, the team went as far as participating in an elaborate voodoo ritual to bring about some of the characters of the past.[122] The reported unexplained taps on their persons and mysterious and sudden chills cannot be experienced by anyone else through a television. However, the audible voices recorded on their equipment (if genuine) are notably eerie. The penchant for hysteria and groupthink notwithstanding, the *Ghost Adventures* team make a good show of Magnolia's now readily accepted supernatural folklore and voodoo superstitions.

Ms. Betty Hertzog, the last living person to have known the Magnolia Plantation as the family residence, openly recalls hearing footsteps in the big house throughout her lifetime, particularly in the upstairs bedrooms, only to find no one present upon investigation. The family superstition, which is recalled on camera not without some humor and with not the least bit of detectable burden, states that when something is lost or moved from where it's supposed to be, Mr. Miller (the former overseer and casualty of the Civil War) has gone off with the object of interest. "Oh, Mr. Miller's got it now," she says, smiling.

Judge Henley Hunter, a descendant of the Hertzog-LeComte alliance, recalls being frightened as a child of going upstairs in the big house. He remembers the day he was playing in the northeastern second-floor bedroom of the big house, where he had presumably been alone for quite a while. Something slapped each of his parents on the back of the neck when they entered the room. The encounter is burned in his memory.[123]

Although the *Ghost Adventures* production might not bring the most convincing portrayal of black magic folklore to the home television screen, the supposed voodoo roots of Magnolia Planation bear mentioning here because scientific investigation has turned up evidence that has led some scholars to conclude the stories of attempted sorcery are more than mere myth. Through a series of archaeological investigations conducted on site in recent years, Dr. Ken Brown, anthropologist at the University of

Houston, claims to have discovered evidence of the practice of voodoo and hexing on individuals at the plantation—and particularly within the quarters areas.

Today, the historic core of Magnolia Plantation is one of two units of the National Park Service's Cane River Creole National Historical Park (the other unit being Oakland Plantation, also located along Louisiana Highway 119 south of Natchitoches, Louisiana). The park includes the overseer's house/slave hospital, a number of slave cabins, the post–Civil War plantation store, the cotton gin barn and a number of fascinating structures spanning more than 150 years of southern plantation history. The extant brick slave cabins alone—occupied as they were through the 1960s—and the intact antebellum cotton screw press are rare surviving fragments of American history unlike anything found nearby. The grounds are open to visitors nearly every day.

The big house at Magnolia Plantation, in contrast, remains in private hands and is only rarely offered for public tour. Sometimes, unsatisfied curiosity does much to preserve the mystique of rare places.

MAGNOLIA PLANTATION
5487 Highway 119
Derry, LA 71416
(318) 356-8441

CHAPTER 8

PAINTED DEFIANCE

SAN FRANCISCO PLANTATION

Once there was nine hundred feet of frontage sculpted in lush greenery, pruned foliage and dancing bright flowers floating in the river breeze. The garden was neatly trimmed and shaped in the latest fashion as it graced the sprawling lawn between the Mississippi River and the big house at the San Francisco Plantation. Here, nectar-thirsty insects and germane suitors pushed aside reserve and went for the spoils. Beyond the botanical gardens stood a landmark sculpted of cypress, brick, slate, painted iron lace and shimmering glass. Now, we can see that time, the ever-eroding river and the United States Army Corps of Engineers removed the garden long ago.

Nonetheless, the landmark that remains is radiant—though now wrapped in protective barbed wire. Beyond the fencing, it is painted in the pastel tones of Victorian splendor and remains dolled up amid the din of the incessant passing oil refinery traffic. The house was grandiose for its time and now is hopelessly wedged between the looming river levee and a sprawling industrial complex on the remaining three sides in its unforgiving present state. The San Francisco big house (for the plantation is no more) appears to stand defiant, a bastion of well-preserved grand domestic architecture amid the ironically decaying industrial complex. Yet the suitors call no more. The house's greatest benefactor today is the oil company that crowds the property with the means to fund its continued quaint existence.

It is true; the contrasts of the scene are stark and obvious to the eye. Yet San Francisco still commands its surroundings. Even the towering catwalks

View of the sculpted garden approaching San Francisco Plantation, pre–1927 flood. *Courtesy of San Francisco Plantation Foundation.*

and vessels of the neighboring plant demand less notice in comparison. Truthfully, it would be easy to assume the plantation derives its name from a glancing resemblance to the painted ladies of San Francisco fame. Nonetheless, the high-style Italianate façade and glimmering paint scheme have no known connection to the West Coast city built along that tragic fault line. And truly, this lady is much more beautiful. For she is no row house. She is the timeless lady of a country estate. San Francisco is found just under forty miles west of New Orleans on the north bank of the River Road, near the rustbelt-like community of Garyville, Louisiana.

In the late 1820s, a free man of color named Elisée Rilieux began acquiring parcels of fertile alluvial land along the lush banks of the Mississippi River. In time, Rilieux had cobbled together a substantial acreage, perhaps constructing some rudimentary improvements for the start of a plantation enterprise. In 1830, he sold the collection of properties to Edmond Bozonier Marmillion, reportedly at a sizeable profit to himself. Edmond Marmillion's family farmed several other properties in the area, but he would eventually choose Rilieux's former investment property as his final home—the home with which to leave a legacy. It is unclear whether there was an earlier house on site, but it seems quite likely that a modest home was erected somewhere near the current residence until means were accumulated for a proper planter's riverside palace.[124] It has been written that Marmillion dreamed of erecting a magnificent home along the waterfront, something that would bedazzle travelers both on land along the River Road and on the river. The emphasis was on impressing passing steamboat traffic.[125] In time, this dream would be accomplished in earnest.

Construction began on Edmond Marmillion's riverside palace around 1853. It is clear Marmillion took pride in the creation of the house from the very beginning. Restoration work on the present big house revealed many timbers with the carved initials "EBM." Beyond his desire to build an exquisite house, Marmillion likely had material cause to begin construction. In 1852, a massive flood inundated the area, likely ruining any prior residence on the plantation. Yet from destruction often comes renewal. As such, the alluvial wash across the already rich farmland yielded a number of bumper sugar crops over the next several years. [126] Those are the kind of crop yields that won't come anymore since the levees got taller—as much a thing of the past as the grand house they financed.

Marmillion was a widower; his wife had died in the early 1840s. At least one source records that she died from tuberculosis, a disease that is thought to also have claimed five of his children. At the time of his wife's passing, he was left with three sons: Pierre Edmond (b. 1826), Antoine Valsin (b. 1827) and Charles Bozonier (b. 1840). However, Pierre Edmond would die the same year as the great flood, and his youngest child, Charles, was habitually in poor health. Edmond's own age was advancing, and he must have known that what he was constructing was a legacy for his strongest heir, Antoine Valsin.[127]

Still, he could not have known that Marmillion Plantation, as it was then known, would be turned over quite so soon. Pierre Edmond Marmillion Sr. died just a few months after the house was completed, while Antoine Valsin was away on a tour of Europe. Antoine Valsin brought back more than hope for the future; he brought back a cultured wife. Legend suggests that Antione arrived home just a day or so after his father's passing. He believed at first glance that the colorful garland and cheery flowers adorning the house were hung on the occasion of his return home and to welcome his new bride—a dramatic homecoming worthy of the grandiose family personality—from present-day Germany. Yet sadly, he would soon learn that the flowers were actually for the occasion of his own father's funeral—a different sort of homecoming altogether.[128]

As soon as the family affairs were settled, Louise Von Seybold Marmillion took possession of her new home with an eye to bring European trends and Germanic influences in interior design into the emerging riverside palace. Her work would especially embrace the budding continental Victorian high styles. The big house may have been originally constructed along more traditional lines on the exterior, but there is no doubt Louise Marmillion had a hand in reimagining its appearance to some degree. Yet her influence on the interior furnishings has left an equally lasting impression. [129] While her touch can be seen everywhere, interestingly it is the gentleman's parlor that she designed for her husband that is quite remarkable. The room is furnished with a painted ceiling indicative of a Bavarian hunting motif that also bears references to the earth's four seasons. Louise Von Seybold also had the Italian muralists paint her face into the scenes again and again—to "watch over her husband always," suggest the contemporary tour guides. [130]

Tour guides will also tell you the house was essentially built to party. The massive folding doors and continuous spaces could be opened up to accommodate large gatherings. To say the house was opulent compared to many in the near vicinity would be an understatement. Folklore suggests the rather plush furnishings and extravagant decorations led Antoine Valsin to remark that he was left "*sans fruscins*" following his wife's renovations. That was an old French term for someone who was virtually penniless. The name stuck (whether the Marmillions liked it or not) but was officially altered to St. Fruscin Plantation for crop ledgers dating to the years just before the Civil War. By 1879, if not sooner, the name had been changed altogether to San Francisco Plantation. [131]

Whoever deserves the credit, the unique appearance of San Francisco Plantation led novelist Francis Parkinson Keyes to coin the phrase "steamboat gothic" in reference to its Corinthian columns and Gothic Revival archways, *bric-à-brac* millwork lacing the gallery and many ornamental and intricately detailed trimmings. Certainly the house does in some ways, and only in the most complimentary manner, resemble the architectural pageantry of high Victorian period steamboats. In appearance, there could have hardly been a less French Creole–looking building in all of Louisiana. [132] Still, there is something inherently Louisianan about its form. The house is a compliment to the exaggerated and fanciful frills of the period, exhibiting intricate decoration for the sake of decoration. Fortunately for Antoine Valsin, his wife's impeccable taste would not leave him without financial wherewithal for very long. Bumper sugar crops were recorded in the years immediately after the completion of the house—it was as though nature itself had approved the fantastic expense of the estate. [133] The flood events that led to the construction of the house paid out in full.

Today, guides tell visitors that the house (at eleven thousand square feet, seventeen rooms and complete with running water) was built for entertainment. San Francisco's floorplan and furnishings seem to reflect

San Francisco Plantation front loggia. *Photograph by W. Ryan Smith.*

this belief. Interestingly, it seems quite probable that Louise Marmillion entertained some of her own native countrymen from time to time, as the River Road area was settled by many German immigrants earlier in the century—lending the longitudinal settlement the epithet of the German coast.[134]

The riverside palace shaped by the Marmillions has been defined by a score of scholars in a great variety of descriptions, from "layer cake" to Italianate and a great variety of evocative determinations between. Certainly the house defies description without firsthand observation—there isn't really any other like it. In contrast with the grandiose exterior, the ground floor is fairly simple in design with common square, plastered brick columns supporting the gallery across the front and halfway back along the east and west ends of the house. The intended public entrance on the front façade is reached by a divided stair that rises from the corners of the house to a central opening on the gallery floor. In its time, the visitors were encouraged to make their way to the house through the extensive and lush front garden—a missing element to the house that must have added untold splendor to the

San Francisco Plantation, rear elevation. *Photograph by W. Ryan Smith.*

moment of arrival at the plantation. Once the visitor was upon the house, he would immediately notice the towering Moorish-domed cisterns flanking the house. Between these architecturally and functionally unique features, grand fluted wooden columns topped with cast-iron Corinthian capitals support the overhanging deck as the dual staircase cascades to the earth below. The overall design is, in the eyes of an architectural historian, "resplendent with scrolls, fluted pillars and Rococo grillwork"—all evocative of the Romantic Period now long passed. The balusters are shaped from turned wood, while the gallery railing is of cast iron—a rarity outside the historic urban Louisiana landscape. The attic is a distinctively Victorian design, which presents a silhouette unique to the house that almost certainly helped inspire the moniker "steamboat gothic."[135]

The second story is constructed of a wood framework filled with brick forming four-inch-thick walls. The exterior of the walls are stucco, while on the interior the finished surface was completed with smoothed plaster.[136] That second-floor portion of the exterior edifice presents what is perhaps the most elegant execution of an otherwise fairly vernacular French Creole

Detail of front elevation of San Francisco Plantation. *Photograph by W. Ryan Smith.*

Cistern detail,
San Francisco
Plantation.
*Photograph by Cheryl
H. White.*

construction technique: *briquetté-entre-poteaux* (brick laid between wooden posts).[137] The vertical segment of the exterior walls adjacent to the attic space is pierced with dozens of fenestrations—paired, louvered shutter-like doors trimmed with ornate brackets all perched under a pronounced and highly decorative Greek Revival cornice. There are also gothic elements present adorning the façade, there are classical elements, there are Creole elements and then there are American elements.[138] This house is unusual in design from beginning to end, yet it is wonderfully executed. In his beautifully written tribute to the River Road plantations, author Richard Sexton has described the house as a "baroque elaboration of a Creole house."[139] There can hardly be a better description made.

The Marmillions' rise in the ranks of the planter class came late in the game. Five years after Louise Marmillion finished her legendary renovations, the United States was ravaging itself in the horrible Civil War. The plantation would survive unscathed, yet young Charles Marmillion would not. Charles served in the esteemed Washington Artillery, a New Orleans–based unit complete with elegant uniforms, polished bronze

Belvedere detail, San Francisco Plantation. *Photograph by W. Ryan Smith.*

cannons, supreme social standing and deep pockets. Still, his service was not only composed of soldiers' balls and grand times in the old Creole city. The Washington Artillery fought in many of the war's most pivotal battles of the eastern theater, incurring more than 150 casualties during the conflict. Charles was himself wounded twice and captured twice, never fully recovering from his wartime experience.[140]

After the war, San Francisco was home to Antoine Valsin and his morose and distant war veteran brother who never married. The marriage of Antoine and Louise brought several daughters to the family, one of whom would die tragically in the house, falling down one of the two elegant wooden stairways and breaking her neck at the bottom of the steps at the tender age of four.[141] The little girl lingered for days but eventually died from complications incurred as a result of the injury. In that time, what could have been done? The uncomfortableness of her condition at that young age is difficult to consider—or maybe it is easier not to.

Antoine Valsin died in 1871 at the early age of forty-four. Charles Marmillion remained at the house, though he was a virtual invalid. Louise would run the plantation with Charles's assistance until 1879, giving up only following Charles's death. Louise must have seen little worth in staying on the estate, or perhaps there was just too much sadness in the house for her to remain there. The Marmillion widow took her three living daughters and moved back to Germany, never to return to Louisiana.[142] The plantation was purchased, completely furnished, by Achille D. Bougère. The new owner immediately changed the name to San Francisco Plantation. Perhaps he was familiar with the architecture of the emerging West Coast city and thought the big house bore some resemblance. Or maybe it was just easier to pronounce or he thought the name trite in the face of the property's potential. The plantation would remain with Bougère until 1905, when he sold the estate, removing all the original furnishings. The furniture was later lost in a fire.[143]

In 1954, the big house at San Francisco Plantation was leased to Mr. and Mrs. Clark Thompson. The couple maintained the home for a while and even opened the mansion to the public on occasion.[144] The Energy Corporation of Louisiana (ECOL Oil) acquired the property in 1973 and began erecting a massive oil refinery complex throughout the former lucrative sugar cane fields.[145] The commercial lure of the riverfront location has maintained the attractiveness of the property throughout its recorded habitation. Evidently, Mrs. Thompson was allowed to remain on the property for a little while. In 1974, Mrs. Thompson, then widowed, moved out of the house. San Francisco

Great Depression–era view of San Francisco Plantation. *Library of Congress, Special Prints and Photographs Collection.*

was by that time in an advanced state of disrepair.[146] For the next three years, the house was restored from top to bottom, literally, as work began with shoring up the expansive slate roof. The New Orleans architectural firm Koch & Wilson oversaw the careful restoration.[147] In 1977, Marathon Oil acquired the property, including the landmark big house.[148] Mercifully, the oil company was determined to save the house.

Folklore has assigned at least three ghosts to San Francisco Plantation: a man and two little girls. Sources indicate the most active specter is identified by name. The postmortem presence of none other than Charles B. Marmillion, the young, morose and traumatized veteran of the American Civil War, is thought by some to remain active at the house. His presence was evidently recorded by the International Society for Paranormal Research in the 1990s and again in a separate 2003 investigation. The apparition is described as a man with a distinctive moustache and reddish-brown hair wearing a long brown coat. This perceptible spirit attributed to Charles is thought to lurk in the bedroom in which he spent much of his invalidity—and where he died. The room is viewable but not always accessible on the public tours. He also is attributed to appearances in the elegant dining room on the first floor, where his "oppressive sensation" overwhelms the occasional visitor to the room.[149]

A prolific source of Charles's continued presence at San Francisco comes from the present-day plantation tour guides.[150] One tour guide reported feeling someone tug her dress while she was within his former bedroom. He is thought to actively open and close doors throughout the house. Yet Charles is not thought alone in his unworldly antics. One visitor to the house claimed to sense an "everlasting supernatural party" on the second-floor loggia on the north side of the house.[151] Presumably, it is the kind of party that evokes multiple specimens. Certainly the stairwell was the cause of much grief and the scene of a tragic accident not long after its construction. On the stairwell where the young Marmillion daughter fell to her death, there is record of an "oppressive" sensation experienced by some visitors, choking and smothering so that it is difficult for those among the living to ascend the stairs.[152]

The above haunting stories carry a sense of understanding with them. But what about two girls playing on the lawn, between the busy River Road, the levee and the modern world all wrapped up at once in an impossible space? There are multiple eyewitness accounts of two little girls playing on the grounds around the big house. Jump rope is mentioned. Or they might be seen having tea under one of the stately oaks gracing the lawn. But who are they? Certainly they exist to some degree, or did. Were they some local's clever idea of a ruse, for it wouldn't be all that hard to fake, or perhaps two forever-young spirits of an untold past? The home was known to host one tragedy involving a young girl, but another? Who is she? The other sisters did not meet tragic fates at an early age. The folklore is intriguing but not easily explained.[153]

When Mrs. Thompson moved out of the San Francisco big house, ECOL Oil, preservationists and the local River Road community took almost immediate action. Among the names commonly cited as instrumental in the effort of saving San Francisco is Sidney Levet Sr., who worked to get the house designated as a National Historic Landmark before it would have been short-sightedly destroyed in a levee-widening project. A massive restoration effort was completed in 1977 at a cost of more than $2 million.[154] The decision was made to bring the house back, as near as possible, through a variety of painstaking scientific means, to the time of its height of elegance, circa 1860. Luckily, there was not much post-Marmillion influence and modifications done to the house over the years that needed to be erased.[155]

A modern kitchen and bathroom were dealt with; additionally, one of the original staircases had been removed. This was restored. The restoration work was true to form, taking every effort to return the house to a snapshot in time. Even historic period modifications were removed. Archaeologists and preservationists used both field and laboratory methods, including fabric testing and paint sequences, to determine original hues and interior design schemes and motifs.[156] Unbelievable ceiling frescoes were recovered through layers of uncooperative paint and touched up only at a minimum to return them as close as possible to their original appearance. The result is a true-to-form replica, an almost seamless restoration of a bygone time.

In 2014, another restoration was completed. Originally, the house's foundation was built on a brick platform approximately one hundred feet square and as much as six feet deep—all to hold up the enormous weight of the mansion.[157] Nonetheless, one of the principal first-floor columns began to sink into the Louisiana muck. The situation put the entire house in jeopardy, with the elegant second-floor porch teetering on disaster. Marathon Oil paid to have the house shored up once again. This time, much of the work completed was conducted below ground and in hidden portions of the house—work never meant to be seen but that nonetheless should help preserve the house for its next 150 years. The house is maintained by the San Francisco Plantation Foundation and is open to the public.

SAN FRANCISCO PLANTATION
2646 Highway 44
Garyville, LA 70051-0950
(985) 535-2341

CHAPTER 9

IRON LACE AND SULLEN WRAITHS

THE MYRTLES PLANTATION

St. Francisville, Louisiana, is a sleepy little community of just about two thousand people today, nestled in a picturesque bend of the Mississippi River in West Feliciana Parish. Situated north of the capital city of Baton Rouge in the area of Louisiana that local folks might call "the boot," St. Francisville occupies an interesting bit of topography—at the beginning of a ridge that runs northward into Tennessee, thereby forming the very southern point of the foothills of the Appalachian Mountains. The fact that St. Francisville exists at all in this unusual location is probably due to this anomaly of the landscape. There can be little doubt that in a state characterized by its lowlands and marshes, a beautiful vista of high bluff on the mighty Mississippi River would have naturally attracted settlement. The Spanish were likely the first European settlers here in the mid-eighteenth century, although of course the land was home to natives for many centuries before. In fact, consistent with the histories of these great plantations, the following is yet another one that draws upon the ancient lore of the first settlers.

Not too far from the main thoroughfare of the small community of St. Francisville, the traveler would find draped in the shadow of moss-covered ancient limbs of oaks a simple yet dramatic façade of a plantation home that has been called one of the most haunted houses in America. The Myrtles Plantation, built in 1796 and today reflecting the significant alterations of the 1830s and beyond, is a structure that seems to always be struggling to find light. Surrounded by a near-forest of massive trees and the kind of lush gardens that naturally flourish in this humid and temperate clime, the home almost seems to be willfully choosing to hide in the landscape. Is it hiding its past? Concealing the secrets of the lives that dominate the plantation-era narrative of the home's history? It has plenty to tell and, yes, plenty to hide. It is a history that is dark but compelling, stained with blood and tears, and echoes yet today of genuine human tragedy and suffering. While the Myrtles Plantation could be considered just another placeholder of antebellum history like dozens of other such institutions across this part of Louisiana, it is unique in both the startling scope of its drama and in the ongoing paranormal and supernatural lore evoked in the imagination at the very mention of its name.

Its moniker of "haunted house" actually derives from some impressive credentialing authorities. After having been the subject of many film documentaries, web and television series with the popular theme of ghost hunting, numerous books (both paranormal and historical) and articles in periodicals across the nation and, indeed, around the world, the home has not ceased to make the news and attract attention. There are literally

Front view of the Myrtles Plantation, shaded with moss-draped trees. *Courtesy of the Myrtles Plantation.*

hundreds of unexplained phenomena and ongoing frights for guests who stay in the location's bed-and-breakfast facilities. The history of the house is a fascinating passage of dark history that begins with its construction in 1796, with the origins of a home destined to become famous for its numerous ghosts that have a penchant for frightening guests even today. It is probably fair to say that most tourists are not seeking history here but haunts. Yet the history is intriguing on its own merit, as well.

David Bradford built the original structure on the site as Laurel Grove Plantation, following receipt of a land grant of six hundred acres from the nearby Spanish colony of Bayou Sara. Persistent legend holds that the land had previously been the site of a Tunica native settlement and a large portion of the land immediately adjacent to the house had been a burial ground for these original inhabitants.[158] Further mystique immediately imprinted on the plantation stems from the fact that Bradford (also known by the nickname of "Whiskey Dave") fled the young United States for the Spanish territory of Louisiana to avoid facing justice for his role in the famous Whiskey Rebellion in Pennsylvania. This rebellion was essentially an act of civil disobedience during the presidency of George Washington to protest a tax on whiskey. The tax had been imposed to raise money to offset the young nation's war debt incurred by independence from Great Britain, and it heavily affected the distillers of western Pennsylvania, the region that Bradford originally called home. Bradford reportedly lived on his Laurel Grove Plantation in virtual hiding for a few years, until he received a pardon from President John Adams in 1799. Bradford's fascinating story of law evasion and eventual presidential pardon is part of a much broader commentary on the early American republic and the nascent efforts to define what would be its expectations for taxation, voice and vote and democratic principles of fairness for its citizens.

Bradford sited the home on a bluff and faced it to the east. It was constructed in a typical Creole cottage-style design that was quite popular in the early nineteenth century across Louisiana, although originally only consisting of four rooms.[159] It is hard to imagine these humble beginnings when seeing the structure today. Following his pardon, Bradford returned to his native Pennsylvania with his family, although he retained ownership of Laurel Grove. Upon his death in 1808, his wife continued to manage the estate through Clarke Woodruff, who had married the Bradfords' daughter Sara and had ties to future president Andrew Jackson. Woodruff ended up fighting alongside Colonel Jackson at the Battle of New Orleans in 1814.[160] Tragedy struck the family in 1823 when Sara Bradford Woodruff died of

The long front gallery of the Myrtles Plantation, again showing its picturesque surrounds. *Courtesy of the Myrtles Plantation.*

yellow fever, a common pestilence to Louisiana throughout the nineteenth century. It was only the first tragedy to be linked to the history of this home, however. There are at least two others that can be historically documented and countless others that exist within the realm of legend alone.

The next chapter in the architectural narrative of the now two-hundred-year-old structure began with the third owners of the property in the mid-nineteenth century. Eventually, the original simple four-room house was expanded to the south, nearly doubling in size, to resemble most closely the structure one sees today from any vantage point. These remarkable improvements were mostly the work of additions undertaken by Ruffin Stirling beginning in 1834. It was Stirling who changed the name of Laurel Grove to Myrtles Plantation, drawn perhaps to the beauty of the many crepe myrtle trees that grew on the property. One of the home's most impressive aesthetic features is a 125-foot veranda that extends the entire length of the structure with its elaborately tooled cast-iron railings. To the eye taking in the façade of the home for the first time, the visual field is dominated by the clapboard exterior, as well as the large symmetrical dormers on the second floor, which reflect an alteration necessary upon the expansion of the house. The rear façade of the existing house has an open loggia with one side facing the gardens, with the addition of dormers that mirror those of the front of the home.[161]

The interior is much like stepping back into a long-lost age, although modern innovations are healthily reflected amid the mixture of its original

The gardens at the Myrtles. *Courtesy of the Myrtles Plantation.*

Creole and later antebellum design. Stepping into the main entrance hall, the space is dominated by a Baccarat crystal chandelier purported to weigh over three hundred pounds (a later addition) but also featuring the original etched stained glass. Many of the rooms on the main first floor of the house feature original imported European marble and original plaster ceiling medallions that are primarily distinguished by the fact that no two of them appear to be the same design.[162]

The paranormal allure of the property dominates the entire history, from the time of the death of Sara Bradford Woodruff to the end of the nineteenth century. Historians cannot verify the often-reported figure of ten murders that occurred on the property, but there is certainly enough tragedy documented in the pages of the Myrtles' history to satisfy anyone seeking the eerie lore that the house and grounds continue to inspire and perpetuate. The plantation's most famous ghost (at least the one that most visitors seem to encounter, or hope to) is that of a slave girl named Chloe who, according to Myrtles legend and lore, was the mistress of Clarke Woodruff. For eavesdropping on a business conversation between Woodruff and other nearby plantation owners, the story goes that Chloe was punished by having her left ear cut off. If that were not painful and humiliating enough, it is said that Woodruff banished the young girl back to the fields and she lost her position as a house slave as a result of her willful curiosity. To be certain, the distinction between field slave and house slave is accurate, with the latter carrying a significant amount more dignity, freedom and privilege.

Of course, the legend does not end with Chloe banished from the house and mutilated. In one of her last acts as a house slave with access to the plantation kitchen, Chloe created a cake recipe that included a small amount of juice from the Louisiana native oleander plant, a toxic poison with properties that act similarly to arsenic. The amount of poison Chloe estimated she used was to be only enough to sicken the family, but instead, two of the Woodruff children reportedly died from ingesting the cake. The legend goes on to say that Chloe was then hanged from a large oak tree on the front lawn of the property, but even in death, Chloe has refused to leave. She repeatedly turns up in accounts of visitors to the home even today who have encountered her apparition or otherwise felt her presence. She may have even been captured in a photograph.

A photograph made on the grounds for insurance purposes revealed what appeared to be the ghostly image of a young girl wearing a turban, standing between the old plantation kitchen and the rear of the Myrtles house as it stands today. Indeed, she may have been captured on film and digital imagery many times since, as the public Internet library of photographs would seem to attest. Neither Chloe nor her fellow ghosts at the Myrtles is afraid of guests, their cameras, cellphones or other ghost-detecting devices. In fact, Chloe and other "spirits" that roam the Myrtles seem to enjoy the frequent encounters with living visitors.[163]

Perhaps more important than any paranormal fascination evoked by the story of Chloe and her tragic end is what the tale has to say about plantation life for slave populations. The fact that the legend places Chloe in the context of "mistress" or "concubine" to the plantation owner Woodruff is reflective of an unfortunate reality for many slave women throughout the antebellum history of the South. The institution of forced servitude left women particularly vulnerable to such exploitation, and women such as Chloe and others like her would not only have lacked any legal recourse, but the act of asserting any resistance would have likely meant only retributive measures. If Chloe's story is true, it is sadly not uncommon in the annals of history. Even if untrue, the legend of Chloe and her circumstances still tells us something quite important about the realities of life for slave populations.

Another ghost with a connection to the broader history of the plantation is purported to be that of William Drew Winter, who lived in the house in the years immediately following the Civil War and was the son-in-law of the Stirlings. Apparently, Winter was shot by a complete stranger in 1871 while standing on the front veranda of the home and staggered inside, where

A photograph that may show a ghostly figure standing between the two buildings. *Courtesy of the Myrtles Plantation.*

he allegedly collapsed and died on the main stairway. Although there are numerous claims in the public imagination about multiple murders that took place on the site, the shooting of Winter is the only one that has been verified in the historical record of the home. Visitors report hearing footsteps on the very stairwell where Winter collapsed and breathed his last.[164]

The stories of Sara Woodruff's fatal end with yellow fever, Chloe's legendary scheme for revenge and her ensuing hanging from an iconic oak tree and the bizarre murder of William Winter on the front gallery of the Myrtles home in broad daylight all do much more than simply spin ghost tales for the curious tourists. Each of these sensational additions to plantation folklore is an important marker within the history of Louisiana, for woven within the colorful tapestry of history are found some signal events and conditions that comment on the realities of life during this era.

Yellow fever was in fact a frequent visitor to Louisiana (as well as many other locales in the temperate and subtropical zones of the United States with large mosquito populations). It claimed thousands of lives in multiple epidemics across the state and across the century in question. The severity of the disease, as well as its dramatic expression in the symptoms of its victims, ultimately drove medical science to discover its root cause. Sara Woodruff in many ways is but a statistic of a chart of contagion that swept across all of Louisiana history. The fact that her personal history is connected to that of the Myrtles Plantation provides the historian another way to expose this crucial aspect of the past to tourists, curiosity seekers and readers.

The conditions of human slavery bring no shortage of tragic and often unbelievable tales of abuse and atrocities. Chloe's legend speaks to the darkest possible heart of that history and highlights in a particular way the plights unique to enslaved women. If her ghost still roams the grounds and halls of the Myrtles Plantation, let that legend be a reminder to all that the allure of the antebellum big house hides an ugly and painful past.

Finally, the tale of the murder of William Winter at the hands of a complete stranger begs that the question of "why" be answered. These are the very types of events that spur the historian and investigative reporter to uncover more of the details. As philosophers might state, the principle of "sufficient reason" drives us to determine the cause of this life cut short. All things, especially events tragic and otherwise unexplainable, demand an explanation. It is a way we order the reality of our environment, manifesting our need to make sense of something nonsensical.

The Myrtles Plantation, haunted as it is by these ghosts of the past, is a veritable museum of lore and legend. Usually shrouded from sunlight, either by intentional landscape design or the ordering of nature, this most famous landmark keeps many secrets, to be sure. Yet if one looks closely enough through the shade of ancient oaks and the thick green of garden environs, there are significant shadows of the past visible to anyone paying attention to the lessons of history.

THE MYRTLES PLANTATION
7747 U.S. Highway 61
St. Francisville, LA 70775
(225) 635-6277
(800) 809-0565

CHAPTER 10

SLAVE TO MASTER

MELROSE PLANTATION

Some landscapes, and only the rarest of human-constructed edifices, seem so draped in folklore and steeped in legend that they still appear almost imaginary even as they are revealed before us. Melrose Plantation, or Yucca,[165] as it was once fancifully known, is one of those exceptional places marked in the course of human events. Fronting the dreamlike Cane River at a slightly acute angle and positioned just 150 feet or so from Louisiana Highway 119, Melrose Plantation is a designated National Historic Landmark—a federal designation for a place of profound significance to the American story—a new-world cathedral of sorts.[166] Yet long before its litany of contemporary recognitions was achieved, Melrose Plantation tantalized the creative. Its legends beckoned the Bayou State's storytellers and culture seekers and begot an entire community of a uniquely Louisianan people. Importantly, Melrose challenges everything we have been taught about plantation history in the southern United States.

Today, the public approach to the plantation demurs its well-documented and long-celebrated significance. The big house is approached not from a grand *allée* of ancient live oaks but from an asphalt lot. From there, a short walking path flanked with dense liriope, Louisiana sandstone and a host of vernacular cottages pulls visitors in from the public carpark east of the big house. Fear not; all of this ordinariness, this subtle nuance of folk life residue, is soon left behind and supplanted by the illusory complications of Melrose Plantation lore. For once the austere approach is trodden, the surreal cultural landscape begins to unveil its sculpted, otherworldly features. In the rising summer sun, the scene is worthy of all the drama of a Victorian copperplate illustrator as mist burns from the earth and fills the atmosphere.

Fittingly, Melrose Plantation traces its human lineage to two legendary figures of colonial Louisiana: Louis Antoine Juchereau de St. Denis and Marie Thérèze Coincoin. Soldier, explorer, statesman, settler, Louis de St. Denis died at Natchitoches Post in 1744, but only after a lifetime of adventure and service to the French colonial government. St. Denis was the life force of the Natchitoches Post and many of the earliest French settlements of Louisiana. Like many men of means at that time, St. Denis was a slaveholder who held a modest number of Africans and Native Americans in bondage—this was well before the grand plantation era required villages of slaves to pull small fortunes out of the ground. Among the estate he left to his children was the enslaved African child Marie Thérèze Coincoin. The two-year-old slave girl was bequeathed to St. Denis's youngest son, Pierre Antoine Juchereau de St. Denis.[167]

Marie Thérèze's father had been brought to French colonial Louisiana through the illicit slave trade sometime in the 1730s.[168] African slaves first began arriving in the area around 1719, just after the formation of the Company of the Indies (a pseudo-private corporation that ran the Louisiana colony for the French monarchy). The Africans were primarily imported from Gambia and Senegal.[169] Contrary to the popular perception of random forays into the African bush, the earliest slaves brought to Louisiana were often chosen for their farming and construction expertise. They were not "unskilled" workers.[170] Nothing was left to circumstance or beyond weighted calculation, for Louisiana was designed to be a profitable venture for the French crown, and slavery would help fuel that economic engine.

As far as is known, Marie Thérèze's life was, until the age of twenty-five, fairly typical of an enslaved domestic servant in early Louisiana. She was encouraged to procreate, though not necessarily marry in the complete Christian sense of the arrangement between a man and woman.[171] This is because if she was married in a Catholic ceremony, her owner could not break up her family under the colonial law known as the *Code Noir*. Undeterred, French colonial slave masters often encouraged their slaves to cohabitate unceremoniously. Thus, the law designed to preserve a tangible thread of humanity for the enslaved was frequently skirted.

By her quarter-century mark, Marie had already given birth to four children. That same year, in 1767, a twenty-three-year-old French émigré named Claude Thomas Pierre Metoyer arrived at Natchitoches Post. What is most notable for this account is that he persuaded Marie Thérèze's owner, by then an aging widower, to lend him the services of Marie Thérèze to live in his home as his own domestic servant.[172] Whether his intentions were rather nefarious from the start or whether their romance bloomed more organically will likely never be known. However, Marie Thérèze soon became much more to Metoyer than a mere domestic servant. Their cohabitation, indeed their love, has become legendary.

Through what appears to have been less of a scandal than one might otherwise imagine, the pair welcomed twins, their first of what would become ten children together, in January 1768. The children were baptized Catholic and given French names directly after Metoyer's own white relatives.[173] This seems to be an indication that Metoyer himself was not embarrassed by the circumstance and fully intended to support the children as his own legitimate offspring in time. Indeed, by the time of the height of the American Revolution, the pair already had seven surviving children together. In a sign of devotion to his life partner, Metoyer had by 1778 acquired enough personal wealth to purchase his longtime companion from St. Denis's descendants and free her from the bonds of slavery forever.

Ironically, now that Metoyer had purchased her freedom, Marie Thérèze left with her children to live on their own for a time. The separation remains sorrowful to this day, heavy on the hearts of their descendants more than two hundred years later. Metoyer married a white widow soon thereafter, but not before setting aside approximately sixty acres for Marie Thérèze and her children to cultivate and live off of in perpetuity. He did this in an age when it would have been completely acceptable, if not predetermined, to cast them off without regard for their continued well-being.[174]

Farm she did. At this point in her life, Marie Thérèze's oldest children were coming of age and were able to help clear the land and work the fields. Marie Thérèze had seen firsthand what ambition could bring someone in colonial Louisiana. Not content with growing subsistence crops to feed her family alone, she began planting tobacco and indigo for profit—cash crops known to advance wealth in the region at that time.[175] In just a few short years, she had petitioned for and received a land grant from the colonial government, began purchasing her own slaves and started a *vacherie* (cattle ranch) with her oldest sons. In complete fulfillment of what likely ranks among the greatest rags-to-riches success stories eighteenth-century Louisiana must have known, Marie Thérèze soon began purchasing the freedom of her own children, one by one. She, of course, had a willing accomplice: her longtime life partner and father of most of her children.[176]

As they came of age, her Metoyer sons began to accumulate vast tracts of land through Spanish colonial grants, worked by their own assemblage of enslaved workers. By the time of her death in 1817, the family's total holdings covered more than ten thousand acres spread across several plantations and *vacheries*. In an ironic twist of history, the Metoyers purchased fifty-eight slaves in just twelve years' time.[177] Slavery was the way of the only world they knew, and Marie Thérèze and her formidable sons would not balk at owning another human to contribute to their own worldly success.

Among their many properties, Marie Thérèze's son Louis Metoyer was able to secure a Spanish land grant along Cane River in 1795. The property would eventually form the nucleus of what would become known as Melrose Plantation. Louis Metoyer's Spanish grant was most unusual in that he was legally still a slave when he received the title to the land. His mother had not yet accumulated enough money to purchase his freedom. Clearly a slave could not own property—or could he? In the remote Natchitoches Post, colonial laws were often loosely interpreted: if there was no victim, there was no crime. In this case, those in the know were not willing to betray Louis's status as owned property (and thus incapable of owning property himself). Rather, he was treated, if not presumed, to be a free man of color (*gens de couleur libres*) by colonial authorities.[178] Certainly his own father was not about to object to the arrangement. Metoyer must have smiled broadly when he thought of his children's unlikely accomplishments. The family's success story came in spite of what most contemporary scholars recognize as general "hostility" to free blacks in the South.[179]

Louis Metoyer constructed what was likely a modest house on the grant and began in earnest to clear the land and cultivate the earth to accumulate more wealth. For the Metoyers, wealth meant more than economic prosperity; wealth would keep the family free. It is unclear whether Marie Thérèze Coincoin ever lived on the property, as is maintained to this day by the local tradition, but it is certainly not beyond the realm of possibility. She would have almost certainly been, at the very minimum, at least familiar with the plantation, as it consisted of approximately 10 percent of their extended family's total acreage. The present big house, an example of a raised Creole cottage, was constructed in 1833 by Louis Metoyer and his son. The family also built the structures that are today known as the Yucca House and the African House.[180]

The former was the first known residence at the plantation and was likely constructed in the second decade of the nineteenth century. The interpreted results of an archaeological investigation suggest an occupation of the site

The Yucca House at Melrose Plantation. *Photograph by W. Ryan Smith.*

after 1810.[181] The so-called Yucca House was a fairly modest residence for an approximately nine-hundred-acre plantation. However, this was not atypical to its time of construction. Before the tremendous wealth of cotton farming was widespread in the area, most of the early plantation homes were constructed in a more utilitarian manner; the enormous Greek temple façades with dominating columns and classical trimmings had not yet begun to dictate Louisiana tastes. The house was built with one floor and consists of only four rooms. It was constructed using traditional Creole methods, including *bousillage*-filled and hand-hewn timber framed walls.

The scholarly term for the construction method used is *poteaux-sur-sol, briquetté-entre-poteaux*. Essentially, the builders used clay gathered from along the riverbank, Spanish moss, lime and occasionally animal hair as an additional binding agent to the muck used to fill the walls between hewn cypress timbers.[182] It was a quintessentially Creole construction technique, reportedly borrowed from the Native Americans in the area, which faded only with the increased availability of cheaply milled lumber in the last half of the nineteenth century.

An oil painting of the Melrose Plantation big house, early twentieth century. *Photograph by W. Ryan Smith.*

The 1830s' big house was built in front of what later became known as Yucca House, forever changing its role from the family's primary residence to a secondary structure, diminished by its replacement in both stature and importance. It is believed to have been used as a hospital for enslaved workers after the construction of the big house.[183] The hexagonal turret-like additions to each end were added at a later date, likely by the Henry family occupation (circa 1884–1970).[184] It is probable the additions were used as *garconnières*, or apartments for the grown, unmarried men and teenage boys of the family, in the old Louisiana tradition. This is interesting in that it presents a tangible relic of the Creolization of an Anglo-American family and French Creole traditions late into the nineteenth century.

The second remaining structure was built early in the occupation of the property and is today known as the African House—so named because of its unusual and exotic appearance that has been traditionally attributed to African architectural influence. While the local tradition of attributing the building's appearance to an African style has stood the test of time, it has been pointed out by some scholars that the house actually has much more in common with post-medieval Norman (French) architecture than it does anything found in Africa. The structure was most probably used for storage

The Melrose Plantation big house. *Library of Congress, Prints and Photographs Division, Historic American Buildings Survey.*

or utilitarian purposes (one account records the possibility that it was once part of a stable). However, the whitewashed, thickly constructed brick walls and the *grilles de défense* (prison-like barred windows) give the building a jail-like persona, which furthers the local tradition that it was used as a lockup for unruly slaves.[185]

The use of the building as a lockup for the enslaved workers is not an impossible theory. However, iron-barred windows were relatively common in French Creole architecture and were usually more effectively employed to keep people *out* (say from a store of wine or other expensive imports) than they were used to keep people *in*. The hand-hewn, dovetail-walled (*pièce-sur-pièce*) upper floor of the African House contains the famous plantation life murals of legendary Louisiana folk artist Clementine Hunter. The paintings depict twentieth-century African American life along Cane River, everyday scenes with amusing detail and enlightening vignettes with a noble quality despite the lack of perspective or depth of observation.

Despite the near unprecedented industrious start, the Metoyer family would reside at Melrose Plantation for only two generations. Henry and Hypolite Herzog purchased the plantation at a sheriff's auction sale in 1847, following a reversal of fortune within the Metoyer family. The brothers

African House, Melrose Plantation, Natchitoches Parish. *Photograph by W. Ryan Smith.*

paid just $8,300 for 2,700 acres of contiguous land and the improvements thereon. The Melrose portion of the estate was literally carved out of a vast tract of land owned by the family, bounded on three of four sides by other Metoyer lands. Only the river itself formed the remaining boundary. The soil here was recognized for its fertility, and it is known to have produced bountiful yields of cotton well into the nineteenth century—long after many farms would have become played out from soil exhaustion and over planting.

In 1884, the plantation was sold again, this time to Joseph Henry, a local planter of means. Henry's intentions for the property were likely to simply add to his collection of productive landholdings, as he did not choose to reside at the aging plantation. Instead, he only made some remedial repairs. At some point in the Henry occupation, the estate was given the name Melrose Plantation. The Henrys, curiously and uncharacteristically, seem to have fully rejected the plantation's past when they chose to rename it after an English abbey highlighted in a Sir Walter Scott poem—that is to say, there could hardly be found a reference further from a French Creole, Catholic, biracial and remote Louisiana existence.[186]

Upon his death at the end of the nineteenth century, Joseph Henry's son acquired Melrose Plantation and moved into the big house with his wife, Carmelite Lou Garrett Henry.[187] Melrose Plantation and the Cane River would never be the same. She began a campaign of unprecedented stewardship that was further fueled by an uncanny affection for all things and all people that made Louisiana what it was. She was so dedicated to preserving Louisiana folklore that "Miss Cammie" Henry and Melrose Plantation were eventually every bit as inseparable terms as the Metoyers and Yucca had once been. Miss Cammie set out to restore the house and the outbuildings. She planted a famously beautiful formal garden, something neglected during the land's long occupation as a profit center and unfortunate abandonment as a formal residence. For many years, the crops were plowed right up to the former residence. Lyle Saxon, a resident writer, described the lush garden in his 1929 work *Old Louisiana* with charming exuberance: "It is the finest garden that I know—a place of riotous blooms and glowing colors. There are more than three acres of flowers."[188]

Saxon had lived in a cabin (known humorously as "the clubhouse" because it was the only place Miss Cammie allowed drinking on the estate) on the property of Melrose Plantation for more than four years when he penned his admiration for her garden. Lyle Saxon, with due respect noted for his remarkable contributions to the preservation and dissemination of Louisiana folklore, was one of many artists to call Melrose Plantation home in the middle of the twentieth century. Over a period of more than fifty years, Miss Cammie cultivated a propensity for attracting all sorts of characters, strangers and locals alike, welcoming them to her home to stay for just a little while or for a lifetime if they so desired. She was a cultured woman and was equally fascinated by the learned and gifted people she came into contact with. To graciously house them all, she turned several outbuildings and former slave cabins across the plantation into comfortable apartments for the multitude of traveling photographers, artists and writers who showed up for her famous hospitality.[189]

Like Bernard of Clairvaux, Miss Cammie loved knowledge for the sake of knowledge and creativity for its promising potential—its service to man. Her unabashed selflessness and generosity to the creative class seems lost today, quaint in a modern time of mistrust, security cameras, mandatory background checks and padlocked properties. Nonetheless, in her time, she let them in and let them stay in droves. Her only "charges," as explained in a 1932 *Dallas Morning News* article, were: 1) You must work. 2) You must not disturb others in their work. 3) You may do as you please, so long as you obey the forgoing two.[190] The late Robert DeBlieux's roster of known former guests included William Faulkner, Lyle Saxon, Harnett Cane, Ross Phares, Rachel Field, Carolyn Ramsey, the ever-colorful Francois Mignon and, of course, folk artist Clementine Hunter, among many others.[191]

Miss Cammie was also a devoted scrapbooker and would compile a veritable treasure-trove of Louisiana history, folklore clippings and photographs over the course of her lifetime. This remarkable collection would later form the cornerstone of the Cammie G. Henry Research Center at Northwestern State University in Natchitoches. In this most unusual manner, through the contributions of Saxon, Hunter, Miss Henry and the many others, Melrose Plantation has both shaped and preserved Louisiana plantation folklore more so than any other one place in the state. Clementine Hunter, a longtime resident of Melrose Plantation, is perhaps the most famous Louisiana primitive artist ever known. Her contribution to African American folk art has inspired countless others, remains the subject of much study and formed the genesis of substantive literary devotionals to African American folk art. Yet the bulk of her work was begun at an advanced age, after a life of labor typical to a black woman in the early twentieth-century American South. Clementine Hunter was sixty-seven years old when she completed her largest commission, the African House murals, between June 8 and July 21, 1955. Francois Mignon talked her into it and commissioned the work.[192]

Beginning in the late 1930s, a number of locals recognized Hunter's talent and began supplying her with quantities of canvas, paint and brushes—as much of it as they could get her to use. This was a form of direct artistic sponsorship that had become so much a part of the Melrose existence.[193] Through the gaze of her eyes and guided by the constructs of her considerable memory, the daubed paint strokes of the African American experience came to life in little figures on colorful canvas vignettes. In that dreamlike world void of geographical perspective, there can be found an all-knowing outlook on southern life. The subjects covered the myriad of her own life experiences, from honkytonks to baptisms in the river, pecan harvests in the fall and church on Sundays. Perhaps she painted simply just so that the rest of us could understand her work.

Clementine Hunter was not without her own eccentricities—another word for the modest level of socially acceptable weirdness allowed good southern people. She once confided to a friend that she had a startling dream in her younger years. In that dream, a voice told her if she chose to

Right: Clementine Hunter, photograph taken at Melrose Plantation. *Collection of Thomas Whitehead*.

Below: *Frenchie Goes to Heaven*, oil painting by Clementine Hunter. *Collection of Thomas Whitehead*.

take a pill at her bedside, it would prolong her life. She awoke, shaken by the dream, only to find a pill on her bedside table. She took the pill and lived to be 101 years old.[194]

Natchitoches Parish is not without its haunts and spectral legends. Lyle Saxon documented one such apparition while working at Melrose. According to local legend, at Lacey Branch plantation, a headless horseman was known to chase pedestrians and even motorists away.[195] Still, in a humorous treatise on the subject, the resident Melrose author also wrote:

> *Of course every old plantation home in Louisiana has at least one ghost. Any that did not would sink into the earth in sheer shame the moment such a fact became known, for a spook is as necessary to a plantation as a legend of the family silver buried in the ground by the faithful slaves the day the damyankees came.*[196]

It may seem an overly humorous discourse on the subject, but nonetheless, there is more than just an ounce of truth in Saxon's argument. It is fairly rare for a Louisiana plantation, but there isn't much chatter about supernatural apparitions at Melrose Plantation. Sure, if you ask enough people or comb through enough papers you may find something on the subject, eventually. Yet Melrose remains different. At Melrose, the residents of its past live on in almost universal regard as local legends, characters of great significance to the Cane River and Louisiana story. Perhaps this is why there is so little need to conjure them from the past. Their relevance remains transcending. Nearly all locals and many distant acquaintances are familiar with their names and at least a portion of their stories.

So perhaps in its own way, Melrose Plantation is forever haunted, forever linked to these unconventional past masters. Though the days have come ceaseless, there is the fresh memory, shared and learned though it is, of Coincoin and Metoyer, Hunter and Saxon and Faulkner and Mignon. As the nation confronts its past with slavery, plantation estates and what it means to be southern, these characters in the southern story are really more relevant today than perhaps ever before. There is found honest disposition in each of them. Through their eyes, it is possible to see the history of the South in a way that southerners can come to know themselves. And so their memories are kept alive, their presence omnipotent. They haunt this place and they define it, more than any physical characteristic or architectural remnant ever could. Perhaps this is why there are no good ghost stories at Melrose. They just aren't needed.

Melrose Plantation is today one of several properties owned and maintained by the Association for the Preservation of Historic Natchitoches (APHN). The APHN was first organized in 1944 as a women's-only club but now operates as an inclusive nonprofit organization based in Natchitoches Parish. The APHN seeks "to promote and preserve an understanding of the rich cultural heritage of Natchitoches and the Cane River area." A fundamental piece of the organization's purpose is to ensure the long-term preservation of Melrose Plantation and a number of historic properties located throughout the region.[197] Melrose Plantation is readily accessible to the public.

MELROSE PLANTATION
3533 Highway 119
Melrose, LA 71452
(318) 379-0055

CHAPTER 11

RÉFLEXION

CONTEMPORARY INTERPRETATIONS OF BEGUILING LANDSCAPES

To us mere mortals, comfortably peering through the sunlit glass in air-conditioned and imported automobiles as we bounce along those ancient lanes now paved, the big houses of old Louisiana excite us in their sudden stillness. "Did you see that old house?" the passenger says, having just caught a glimpse of something seemingly ancient through a break in blurring foliage, scattergun-pierced road signs and miles of ubiquitous rural decay as the car sweeps across the lumpy parish road. "No, I guess I missed it," says the driver, matter of fact like and unassuming. At once, the old estate is again forgotten by both. This is just as well, for the house was robbed of its firebox mantels, gasolier fixtures, parlor moldings and structural dignity long ago.

Then there are the old house pilgrims, a graying and dwindling group of true enthusiasts, girded with insect repellant, sun visors, parish tourism bureau travel brochures and plenty of plastic-bottled spring water. Whole weeks are set aside to ramble through the once-private *chambres* of lives long passed on. To gaze at the idealized way things were before text messaging killed written and verbal communication in one fatal blow, before daytime television forever buried common courtesy and before the proliferation of yoga studios made it reasonable to wear exercise ensembles in public. In those days, women were women, tea was expensive and life was mercifully short.

Now, architectural historians and preservationists admire these homes for their physical being, having lasted a great number of years along the timeline of history. Scientists determine the species and age of the wood used in the roof truss construction and count the number of sidelights chosen to illuminate the entry of an American central hall plan house. The big houses are studied in prodding isolation, in unmerciful and revealing detail that leaves nothing to the imagination. They are measured and drawn, cross-sectioned and illustrated for full view. The plantation big houses are a puzzle to be solved, a tangible folklore to be demystified and splayed open for the benefit of an insatiable earthly knowledge. There are hand-wrought nails that must be counted and measured. The paint layers are recorded and cataloged. The past must be unpackaged and brought to bear under the ceaseless enquiry of the all-knowing present.

Many find the painful histories associated with them—cruelty, war, famine, poverty and extravagance lost—to be provocateurs of influence among the spirits of the dead. Plantations conjure images of harsh masters whipping their slaves and heinous voodoo rituals seeking revenge on the unsuspecting. Many plantations bore witness to incredible violence through war or rebellion. It is easy to imagine that if the supernatural realm really does hold secrets from us, they are forever locked among the knowing walls of the plantation big house and the slave cabin, forever juxtaposed in the landscape of human slavery.

To others, the Louisiana big house simply symbolizes a repressive past—obtrusive monuments to the tormenters of men, women and children held in bondage through the circumstance of their own birth. This view is increasingly true among these latest generations, whether they can trace ancestral slavery in their own roots or not. Even still, so many others are embarrassed to be associated with them, even geographically. To be southern is to hold an apology in your pocket, tucked away for rapid use when socially required. Among their ranks are many academics who eagerly pursue plantation cultural landscape studies, African Diaspora archaeology where reports have shown the deed of sweeping a yard clean in the plantation quarters was an open act of defiance against planter tyranny. Though often overzealous in their interpretations, they are largely correct. Truly, the degree of inhumanity that was required for their very construction, let alone daily operation, is revolting.

Can these houses ever be pardoned of the sins of their creators? How else can the healing begin? To raze these empty houses, through neglect or forcible means, will not erase the legacy of slavery nor unbind the ghosts of the troubled generations long past. Truly, generations come and go. New customs rise and traditional beliefs wane. But the past is frozen as it was, in both darkness and in light. In this way, the finite resource of the remaining Louisiana plantation big houses is a shared responsibility, just as is the cleanliness of the rural highways that connect them in the crudest sense or the preservation of the wetland habitats in the now most universally accepted sense. Until that time is realized, they will remain the unforgiven. Stately in a casual world, cursed among a self-righteous culture, decaying in an uncompromising climate, humbled by technological advance.

In some ways, it is the political entity of Louisiana itself that encourages the stagnation and rot. The state is widely noted for its peculiarity in terms of its body of laws. Among them is the old French ideal of forced heirship that requires property, that is to say the enduring interests of deceased parents, be divided evenly among their children under a variety of conditions. Likewise, the legacy of the Louisiana plantation home is a sort of forced heirship upon its citizens.

The big house marks the off-limits place among vast acres of toil by nameless droves who labored in the sun and worked the dark alluvium to build fantastic wealth for but a few others. The big house marks the place of uncomfortable pride in the hearts of its creator's descendants. For the many who share the blood of both the enslaved and the landed gentry (a uniquely New World and largely Louisianan trait), there should be no clearer place of reflection, where the past has been made prologue, albeit columned and stately. The Louisiana big house is a physical place to reflect on how the "peculiar institution" once begat an entirely new culture.

Louisiana plantation big houses, whether a raised cottage or a grandiose classical temple replica (or some whimsical Creolized hybrid in between), are a lasting remnant of so many lives before our time—even as that time moves forward. They are the deposit of Louisiana culture, eternal glimpses at an agrarian society waning long before many of them were even conceived, let alone constructed. Feudal fiefdoms transported to the New World, they are at once foreign and uniquely native. They are now the residue of a culture no less ancient than that of the classical Greeks. It is this shared history of its citizens, for the greater majority of Louisianans were born in Louisiana, as their parents were and their own children were or likely will be. They stand in defiance of time itself, the slipping of days into an uncertain future. In all probability, they will stand long after many of us return to our own creator.

What, then, will be the fate of the Louisiana big house? Some two hundred years removed, whom among us will save them? The big houses have survived war and weathering, hurricanes and invasive insect infestations, social upheaval, unmerciful architectural modifications, benign neglect, cultural relativism and outright vandalism. In a sense, they are not immortal because they will not always be physically present. Certainly, all things built by man will come down in time. Nonetheless, should they stand infinitely with the state, there remains scattered throughout its rural districts a tangible common ground to remember where so many Louisianans trace their own lineage. In this way, they are immortal. Yet they must remain with us, seared in our memory as places of shared pain and grandeur, pageantry and merciless cruelty. Places where those unimaginable yet everyday lives were witnessed, where tangible folklore remains beyond the narrative pages. Therein, spirits of the past are stored, preserved in homage to humanity.

The Louisiana big houses remain with us always, stoic reflections of past lives and legacies. They are the reliquaries of North America's most complicated heritage. Though our names don't often match that of their creators, they universally belong to all of us. As such, they deserve, above anything, the charitable mercy of preservation.

Notes

Chapter 2

1. Russell, *Pictures of Southern Life*, 108.
2. Poesch and Bacot, *Louisiana Buildings*, 140.
3. Blanchard, *Louisiana's Sugar Palace*, 24.
4. Ibid.
5. Sternberg, *Along the River Road*, 175.
6. Blanchard, *Louisiana's Sugar Palace*, 35.
7. Ibid.
8. U.S. Government, *Annual Report of the Commissioner of the General Land Office*, 1887, 567.
9. United States Congress, *Congressional Globe*, vol. XIV, 114.
10. Poesch and Bacot, *Louisiana Buildings*, 142.
11. Theriot, *La Meilleure de la Louisiane*, 192.
12. Sternberg, *Along the River Road*, 175.
13. Sillery, "Folklore or Fakelore."
14. Ibid.

Chapter 3

15. Levatino, *Past Masters*, 3.
16. Ibid.
17. Sexton, *Vestiges of Grandeur*, 15. The German immigrants settled primarily along the river above (upstream or west of) New Orleans. Eventually, the area became known as the German Coast. Many families fully embraced assimilation to French culture and became quite prosperous.
18. Levatino, *Past Masters*, 4–5.

19. Malone and Malone, *Louisiana Plantation Homes*, 40; Sexton, *Vestiges of Grandeur*, 21.
20. Levatino, *Past Masters*, 7.
21. Ibid., 7, 12. Until the Seventeenth Amendment in 1913, U.S. senators were elected by state legislatures.
22. Pascoe, *Louisiana's Haunted Plantations*, 100.
23. Levatino, *Past Masters*, 13; Sexton, *Vestiges of Grandeur*, 21. *Garconnières* were typically used as living quarters for teenage and early adult children of the family, whether built as a separate freestanding structure or the wing of a larger house (Edwards and Bellay de Verton, *Creole Lexicon*, 107).
24. Levatino, *Past Masters*, 13–15.
25. Malone and Malone, *Louisiana Plantation Homes*, 40.
26. Levatino, *Past Masters*, 19.
27. Smith, *Southern Queen*, 30.
28. Ibid.
29. Levatino, *Past Masters*, 20.
30. Smith, *Southern Queen*, 30.
31. Ibid., 31.
32. Ibid.; Levatino, *Past Masters*, 20–22; Rodriguez, *Encyclopedia of Slave Resistance*, vol. II, 612.
33. Levatino, *Past Masters*, 23.
34. Ibid., 25.
35. Ibid.
36. Ibid., 27, 29.
37. Pascoe, *Louisiana's Haunted Plantations*, 100.
38. Levatino, *Past Masters*, 32–34
39. Ibid., 34–35.
40. Louisiana Supreme Court, *Reports of Cases Argued*; Levatino, *Past Masters*, 36–38.
41. Pascoe, *Louisiana's Haunted Plantations*, 100; Levatino, *Past Masters*, 36–38.
42. Levatino, *Past Masters*, 37.
43. Ibid., 41–42.
44. Ibid., 43–42; Sexton, *Vestiges of Grandeur*, 21.
45. Levatino, *Past Masters*, 45–46.
46. Brown, *Stories from the Haunted South*, 129; Sexton, *Vestiges of Grandeur*, 102.
47. Pascoe, *Louisiana's Haunted Plantations*, 103; Saxon, *Old Louisiana*, 294; *New Orleans Advocate*, October 31, 2016.
48. Brown, *Stories from the Haunted South*, 129.
49. Sillery, *Haunting of Louisiana*, 46.
50. Pascoe, *Louisiana's Haunted Plantations*, 105.
51. Jean Lafitte biographer Lyle Saxon noted the many generations–old folktale of Lafitte's buried treasure encompasses an approximately one-thousand-mile stretch of coastline of the Gulf of Mexico, including countless bays, inlets, rivers and bayous from Texas to Florida. See Sillery, *Haunting of Louisiana*, 48.
52. Pascoe, *Louisiana's Haunted Plantations*, 104.

53. Sillery, *Haunting of Louisiana*, 47–48, 50; Malone and Malone, *Louisiana Plantation Homes*, 40.
54. Pascoe, *Louisiana's Haunted Plantations*, 107.
55. Sternberg, *Along the River Road*, 117.
56. *New Orleans Advocate*, October 31, 2016.

Chapter 4

57. Mark Twain, *Life on the Mississippi* (New York: American Publishing Company, 1899), 310.
58. Sternberg, *Along the River Road*, 279.
59. Poesch and Bacot, *Louisiana Buildings*, 88.
60. Ibid., 280.
61. Roman Family Papers, Louisiana Research Collection, Tulane University.
62. Sternberg, *Along the River Road*, 280.
63. Ibid.
64. National Park Service, "The River Road," *The History and Culture of Southeastern Louisiana*.
65. National Park Service, Field Records, Historic American Buildings Survey.
66. Kenneth Gravois, "History of Sugarcane Research in Louisiana," LSU College of Agriculture, 2012.
67. Leonard Gianessi and Ashley Williams, "Herbicides Saved Louisiana Sugarcane Production Following Shortages of Labor for Weeding," U.S. Pesticides Benefit Case Study, 2011.
68. Sternberg, *Along the River Road*, 281.

Chapter 5

69. Sternberg, *Along the River Road*, 244.
70. Castaldi, *Nottoway Plantation*, 6–7.
71. John H. Randolph Papers, Louisiana and Lower Mississippi Valley Collections, LSU Library.
72. Sternberg, *Along the River Road*, 244.
73. John H. Randolph Papers.
74. Marshall, "Legacy of Henry Howard."
75. "Nottoway Plantation," KnowLA, Louisiana Endowment for the Humanities.
76. Castaldi, *Nottoway Plantation*, 24.
77. United States Census, 1860.
78. Fiske, "Skeptical Reporter's Louisiana Ghost Story."
79. John H. Randolph Papers.
80. Castaldi, *Nottoway Plantation*, 44.

81. John H. Randolph Papers.
82. Fiske, "Skeptical Reporter's Louisiana Ghost Story."
83. Nottoway Plantation, October 28, 2009.
84. John H. Randolph Papers.

Chapter 6

85. U.S. National Park Service, Cane River National Heritage Area: Cherokee Plantation.
86. U.S. Government, *Biographical Directory of the United States Congress.*
87. Mayeux, *Earthen Walls, Iron Men*, 275.
88. Williams, *Dueling in the Old South*, 6.
89. Ibid.
90. Isbell, "Blood and Honor."
91. Mayeux, *Earthen Walls, Iron Men*, 276.
92. Ibid.
93. Ibid.
94. U.S. National Park Service, Cane River National Heritage Area: Cherokee Plantation.
95. Historic American Buildings Survey, Cherokee Plantation.
96. Cherokee Plantation interviews, January–February 2017.

Chapter 7

97. Keel, Miller and Tiemann, *Comprehensive Subsurface Investigation of Magnolia Plantation*, 18.
98. See Byrd, *Colonial Natchitoches*, especially 59–97, for a well-composed and concise study of the economy of the frontier outpost.
99. Keel, Miller and Tiemann, *Comprehensive Subsurface Investigation of Magnolia Plantation*, 18–19.
100. Hunter, *Magnolia Plantation*, 2.
101. Keel, Miller and Tiemann, *Comprehensive Subsurface Investigation of Magnolia Plantation*, 18–19; Malone, "Magnolia Plantation Overview," 2–3.
102. Hunter, *Magnolia Plantation*, 7.
103. Keel, Miller and Tiemann, *Comprehensive Subsurface Investigation of Magnolia Plantation*, 18–19.
104. Ibid.; 1860 U.S. Slave Schedule.
105. Hunter, *Magnolia Plantation*, 9.
106. During the 1850s, there was much debate, through journals such as *Southern Planter* and *Southern Cultivator*, about southern planters' responsibilities toward their enslaved workers. Primitive slave housing of prior generations was widely held

to be substandard and inhumane. Such were the varying degrees of humanity during the period. See Clifton Ellis's work "Building for 'Our Family,' Black and White," 143, in Ellis and Ginsburg, *Cabin, Quarter, Plantation*.

107. Hunter, *Magnolia Plantation*, 9.
108. Cloutierville residents voted 144 to 3 against secession. See Malone, "Magnolia Plantation Overview"; Dollar, "Red River Campaign," 427.
109. Keel, Miller and Tiemann, *Comprehensive Subsurface Investigation of Magnolia Plantation*, 20.
110. Hunter, *Magnolia Plantation*, 25.
111. Smith and Graham, "Military Heritage Archaeological Resource Assessment," 202; Gould, *History of the First—Ninth—Twenty-Ninth Maine Regiment*, 409.
112. Dollar, "Red River Campaign," 425–27.
113. Smith, *Life and Letters of Thomas Kilby Smith*, 127; Dollar, "Red River Campaign," 427; Smith and Graham, "Military Heritage Archaeological Resource Assessment," 202.
114. Hunter, *Magnolia Plantation*, 26; Joyous Coast Foundation, *Images of America: Natchitoches*, 61. One tradition claims that Mr. Miller was buried near the front steps of the house, where he had fallen. As unlikely as this seems, there was some precedent. The LeComte family's prized racehorse, Flying Dutchman, was known to have been buried in the area.
115. Breedlove, "Bermuda/Oakland Plantation," 45.
116. Bass, et. al., *Magnolia Plantation Overseer's House*, 11.
117. Ibid.
118. Betty Hertzog, Oral History and Ethnographic Interviews.
119. Bass, et. al., *Magnolia Plantation Overseer's House*, 1–2; Hunter, *Magnolia Plantation*, 26.
120. Ambrose Hertzog, Oral History and Ethnographic Interviews.
121. Ibid.
122. *Ghost Adventures*, "Magnolia Plantation."
123. Hunter, personal communication.

Chapter 8

124. San Francisco Plantation Foundation, *Return to Elegance*, 2; Southall, *Haunted Plantations of the South*.
125. San Francisco Plantation Foundation, *Return to Elegance*, 1; Higginbotham, *Marvelous Old Mansions*, 69. There are a number of sources that suggest Marmillion sought inspiration for the house from the passing steamboat traffic on the river. Certainly the house little resembles the typical Creole habitation of its day.
126. San Francisco Plantation Foundation, *Return to Elegance*, 2, 27.
127. Southall, *Haunted Plantations of the South*; San Francisco Plantation Foundation, *Return to Elegance*, 2.
128. Pascoe, *Louisiana's Haunted Plantations*, 82.

129. San Francisco Plantation Foundation, *Return to Elegance*, 1–2; Malone and Malone, *Louisiana Plantation Homes*, 132.
130. Sexton, *Vestiges of Grandeur*, 107. The guide took much delight in describing how the many faces of Louise follow the gentlemen around the room.
131. San Francisco Plantation Foundation, *Return to Elegance*, 1–2. You will find likely as many translations of this phrase and versions of the naming of the plantation as the sources you consult. Other translations include: "without a penny in my pocket," "without your last cent," "without your last shirt" or "without anything left." Even still, the intent of the meaning is clear: the renovation and furnishing of the house cost the Marmillions dearly.
132. Ibid., 1.
133. Ibid., 2.
134. Ibid., 2; Pascoe, *Louisiana's Haunted Plantations*, 83.
135. National Park Service, National Register of Historic Places Inventory Form: San Francisco Plantation; Butler, *Pelican Guide to Plantation Homes of Louisiana*, 29; Poesch and Bacot, *Louisiana Buildings*, 152. The elevated cisterns, dressed to resemble Moorish minarets, were a nineteenth-century novelty in Louisiana. Beyond their striking appearance, the aboveground positioning provided adequate water pressure to the interior plumbing of the house.
136. San Francisco Plantation Foundation, *Return to Elegance*, 27.
137. The brick between posts construction method was certainly a step up from the more rudimentary *bousillage* fill. Nonetheless, clapboard siding was routinely used to cover it, signifying its place as a framing element and not a finished surface. At San Francisco, the siding is covered in stucco, with the large frames painted and exposed. See Edwards and Bellay de Verton, *Creole Lexicon*, 34–35.
138. National Park Service, National Register of Historic Places Inventory Form: San Francisco Plantation.
139. Sexton, *Vestiges of Grandeur*, 86.
140. U.S. National Park Service, "NPS Soldiers and Sailors System"; San Francisco Plantation Foundation, *Return to Elegance*, 2. Guides at San Francisco are quick to point out that Charles must have suffered from what is today commonly known as post-traumatic stress disorder.
141. Pascoe, *Louisiana's Haunted Plantations*, 84–85, 90.
142. Ibid., 2.
143. Ibid., 3.
144. Ibid., 3.
145. Ibid., 85.
146. San Francisco Plantation Foundation, *Return to Elegance*, 4.
147. Sexton, *Vestiges of Grandeur*, 86; San Francisco Plantation Foundation, *Return to Elegance*, 26.
148. Pascoe, *Louisiana's Haunted Plantations*, 85.
149. Ibid., 86, 89.
150. Curiously, the author's guide made not a single reference to the supernatural while the author visited, nor did anyone else present at the time.

151. Pascoe, *Louisiana's Haunted Plantations*, 87–88.
152. Ibid., 87.
153. Ibid., 89—90; Southall, *Haunted Plantations of the South*.
154. San Francisco Plantation Foundation, *Return to Elegance*, 25; Pascoe, *Louisiana's Haunted Plantations*, 85; Sexton, *Vestiges of Grandeur*, 86; Higginbotham, *Marvelous Old Mansions*, 70.
155. San Francisco Plantation Foundation, *Return to Elegance*, 25.
156. Ibid., 25.
157. National Park Service, National Register of Historic Places Inventory Form: San Francisco Plantation.

Chapter 9

158. Sillery, *Haunting of Louisiana*, 17.
159. Pascoe, *Louisiana's Haunted Plantations*, 12.
160. U.S. National Park Service, "Myrtles Plantation."
161. Ibid.
162. Ibid.
163. Sillery, *Haunting of Louisiana*, 21.
164. Ibid., 24.

Chapter 10

165. Research suggests the name "Yucca" first appears only in the 1930s, through the imagination and wit of legendary resident François Mignon, who had a bent for naming things. Whitehead, personal communication.
166. According to the National Historic Landmarks Program, National Historic Landmarks are "nationally significant historic places…[that] possess exceptional value or quality in illustrating or interpreting the heritage of the United States. There are a little more than 2,500 historic places so designated." www.nps.gov/nhl.
167. Mills, *Forgotten People*, 5–6; Gould, et. al., *Natchitoches and Louisiana's Timeless Cane River*, 82.
168. Mills, *Forgotten People*, 2–3.
169. Sexton, *Vestiges of Grandeur*, 15. Elsewhere, it has been suggested that the name Coincoin most closely translates to Kō Kwē, from a name used for second-born daughters to families of the coastal district of Togo, some eight hundred miles east of Senegal and Gambia (see Mills, *Forgotten People*, 3).
170. Sternberg, *Along the River Road*, 6; Sexton, *Vestiges of Grandeur*, 15.
171. Mills, *Forgotten People*, 7–9.
172. Ibid., 5.
173. Ibid., 11, 22; Gould, et. al., *Natchitoches and Louisiana's Timeless Cane River*, 82.

174. This freedom was not transferrable to her half-French children, who legally remained the property of their own father. Her first four children remained the property of another estate. See Mills, *Forgotten People*, 26–28.

175. Mills, *Forgotten People*, 31.

176. Ibid., 33–34.

177. Ibid., 64, 66. The colonial grants could be generous, sometimes requiring only that the landowner maintain a public road along the riverbank and tend to the natural levee for flood protection (Sternberg, *Along the River Road*, 42).

178. Mills, *Forgotten People*, 54.

179. Ellis and Ginsburg, *Cabin, Quarter, Plantation*, 69.

180. Gould, et. al., *Natchitoches and Louisiana's Timeless Cane River*, 83.

181. See MacDonald, Morgan, Handley, et. al., "Archaeology of Local Myths."

182. Edwards and Bellay de Verton, *Creole Lexicon*, 32. The recipe for *bousillage* seems to vary between locations across the state. Closer to the coast, *bousillage* may also contain crushed seashells or mussel shells, as can be observed at Destrehan Plantation in St. Charles Parish, Louisiana.

183. Mills, *Forgotten People*, 121; NPS, National Register of Historic Places.

184. www.melroseplantation.org/history; NPS, National Register of Historic Places.

185. Edwards and Bellay de Verton, *Creole Lexicon*, 4, 112; Vlach, *Back of the Big House*, 85–86; NPS, National Register of Historic Places.

186. Gould, et. al., *Natchitoches and Louisiana's Timeless Cane River*, 82; Mills, *Forgotten People*, 249; Whitehead, personal communication.

187. Gould, et. al., *Natchitoches and Louisiana's Timeless Cane River*, 82; Saxon, *Old Louisiana*, 364.

188. Saxon, *Old Louisiana*, 364.

189. Whitehead, personal communication; Gould, et. al., *Natchitoches and Louisiana's Timeless Cane River*, 82.

190. *Dallas Morning News*, March 26, 1932.

191. Gould, et. al., *Natchitoches and Louisiana's Timeless Cane River*, 82, 85.

192. Shiver and Whitehead, *Clementine Hunter*, ix.

193. Ibid., ix, 2. In his work, *Clementine Hunter: Her Life and Art*, longtime friend Thomas Whitehead jokes that he doesn't think Clementine Hunter ever actually purchased any paint; it was always waiting for her when she needed it.

194. Whitehead, personal communication.

195. Saxon, Tallant and Dreyer, *Gumbo Ya-Ya*, 272.

196. Ibid., 271.

197. www.melroseplantation.org/history.

BIBLIOGRAPHY

Association for the Preservation of Historic Natchitoches. "Melrose Plantation: History." www.melroseplantation.org/history.

Bass, Robert A., et. al. *Magnolia Plantation Overseer's House Historic Structure Report.* Atlanta: National Park Services Cultural Resources Southeast Region, 2004.

Blanchard, Jim. *Louisiana's Sugar Palace: Houmas House Plantation and Gardens.* N.p., 2014.

Breedlove, Carolyn. "Bermuda/Oakland Plantation, 1830–1880." Master's thesis, Northwestern State University of Louisiana, 1999.

Brown, Alan. *Stories from the Haunted South.* Jackson: University of Mississippi Press, 2004.

Butler, Anne. *The Pelican Guide to Plantation Homes of Louisiana.* Gretna, LA: Pelican Publishing Company, 2009.

Byrd, Kathleen M. *Colonial Natchitoches: Outpost of Empires.* Bloomington, IN: Xlibris Corporation, 2008.

Castaldi, Robin Summers. *Nottoway Plantation: The South's Largest Antebellum Mansion.* N.p.: Nottoway Properties, 2013.

Dollar, Susan. "The Red River Campaign, Natchitoches Parish, Louisiana: A Case of Equal Opportunity Destruction." *Louisiana History, The Journal of the Louisiana Historical Association* 43, no. 4 (Fall 2002).

Edwards, Jay Dearborn, and Nicolas Kariouk Pecquet Bellay de Verton. *A Creole Lexicon: Architecture, Landscape, People.* Baton Rouge: Louisiana State University Press, 2004.

Ellis, Clifton, and Rebecca Ginsburg. *Cabin, Quarter, Plantation: Architecture and Landscapes of North American Slavery.* New Haven, CT: Yale University Press, 2010.

Fiske, Molly Hennessy. "A Skeptical Reporter's Louisiana Ghost Story." *Los Angeles Times*, August 29, 2016.

Ghost Adventures. "Magnolia Plantation." Produced and directed by Zak Bagans, et. al. 44 min. 2008.

Goeldner, Paul. "Nomination Form: San Francisco Plantation Home." National Register of Historic Places, National Park Service, 1974.

Gould, John Mead. *History of the First—Ninth—Twenty-Ninth Maine Regiment*. Portland, ME: Stephen Berry, 1871.

Gould, Philip, Richard Seale and Robert DeBlieux, et. al. *Natchitoches and Louisiana's Timeless Cane River*. Baton Rouge: Louisiana State University Press, 2002.

Hertzog, Ambrose. Oral history by Dayna Bowker Lee. July 25, 2015, Magnolia Plantation Store, Highway 119, Derry, LA, transcript. Oral History and Ethnographic Interviews with Traditionally Associated People of Cane River Creole National Historical Park.

Hertzog, Betty. Oral history by Dayna Bowker Lee. August 14, 2015, Magnolia Plantation Store, Highway 119, Derry, LA, transcript. Oral History and Ethnographic Interviews with Traditionally Associated People of Cane River Creole National Historical Park.

Higginbotham, Sylvia. *Marvelous Old Mansions: And Other Southern Treasures*. Winston-Salem, NC: John F. Blair, Publisher, 2000.

Hunter, Judge Henley Alexander. *Magnolia Plantation: A Family Farm*. Natchitoches, LA: Northwestern State University Press, 2005.

———. Personal communication, January 20, 2017, Natchez, LA.

Isbell, Terry. "Blood and Honor: Duel on the Cane." *Natchitoches Parish Magazine* 1, reprinted at usgwarchives.net.

Joyous Coast Foundation. *Images of America: Natchitoches*. Charleston, SC: Arcadia Publishing, 2003.

Keel, Bennie C., Christina E. Miller and Mark A. Tiemann. *A Comprehensive Subsurface Investigation of Magnolia Plantation*. Tallahassee, FL: National Park Service Southeast Archaeological Center, 1999.

Levatino, Madeline. *Past Masters: The History & Hauntings of Destrehan Plantation*. Destrehan, LA: Levatino & Barraco, 1991.

Louisiana Supreme Court. *Reports of Cases Argued and Determined in the Supreme Court of Louisiana*. Vol. II. New Orleans, LA: F.F. Hansell & Brothers, 1895.

MacDonald, Kevin, David Morgan and David W. Handley, et. al. "The Archaeology of Local Myths and Heritage Tourism: The Case of Cane River's Melrose Plantation." In *A Future for Archaeology: The Past in the Present*. Edited by Robert Layton, Stephen Shennan and Peter Stone. London: University College London Press, n.d.

Malone, Ann Patton. "The Magnolia Plantation Overview." Manuscript on file, Cane River Creole National Historical Park, Natchitoches, Louisiana, 1996.

Malone, Paul, and Lee Malone. *Louisiana Plantation Homes: A Return to Splendor*. Gretna, LA: Pelican Publishing Company, 2001.

Marshall, Keith. "The Legacy of Henry Howard." *New Orleans Times Picayune*, June 1, 2015.

Mayeux, Steven. *Earthen Walls, Iron Men: Fort DeRussy, Louisiana and the Defense of the Red River*. Knoxville: University of Tennessee Press, 2007.

Mills, Gary B. *The Forgotten People: Cane River's Creoles of Color*. Baton Rouge: Louisiana State University Press, 1977.

New Orleans Advocate, October 31, 2016.

Pascoe, Jill. *Louisiana's Haunted Plantations*. Baton Rouge, LA: Irongate Press, 2004.

Poesch, Jessie, and Barbara Bacot, eds. *Louisiana Buildings 1720–1940: The Historic American Buildings Survey*. Baton Rouge: Louisiana State University Press, 1997.

Randolph, John H. *Collected Papers*. New Orleans, LA: Tulane University Library & Archives.

Rodriguez, Junius P. *Encyclopedia of Slave Resistance and Rebellion*. Vol. II. Santa Barbara, CA: Greenwood Press, 2007.

Russell, Sir William Howard. *Pictures of Southern Life: Social, Political, and Military*. New York: James G. Gregory, 1861.

San Francisco Plantation Foundation. *Return to Elegance: San Francisco Plantation House*. Grayville, LA: San Francisco Plantation Foundation, n.d.

Saxon, Lyle. *Old Louisiana*. New York: Century Company, 1929.

Saxon, Lyle, Robert Tallant and Edward Dreyer. *Gumbo Ya-Ya: A Collection of Louisiana Folk Tales*. New York: Bonanza Books, 1984.

Sexton, Richard. *Vestiges of Grandeur: The Plantations of Louisiana's River Road*. San Francisco: Chronicle Books, 1999.

Shiver, Art, and Tom Whitehead. *Clementine Hunter: Her Life and Art*. Baton Rouge: Louisiana State University Press, 2012.

Sillery, Barbara. "Folklore or Fakelore: A Trio of Haunted Plantations." *Louisiana Life*, 2011.

———. *The Haunting of Louisiana*. Gretna, LA: Pelican Publishing Company, 2006.

Smith, Thomas Ruys. *Southern Queen: New Orleans in the Nineteenth Century*. London: Continuum International Publishing Group, 2011.

Smith, Walter George. *Life and Letters of Thomas Kilby Smith*. New York: G.P. Putnam's Sons, 1898.

Smith, W. Ryan, and Suzanne Graham. "Military Heritage Archaeological Resource Assessment and Survey of the Cane River National Heritage Area." Natchitoches, LA: Cane River National Heritage Area, 2010.

Southall, Richard. *Haunted Plantations of the South*. Woodbury, MN: Llewellyn Publications, 2015.

Sternberg, Mary Ann. *Along the River Road: Past and Present on Louisiana's Historic Byway*. Baton Rouge: Louisiana State University Press, 2013.

Theriot, Jude. *La Meilleure de la Louisiane*. Cambridge, UK: Cambridge University Press, 2009.

United States Congress. *The Congressional Globe: Sketches and Debates of the Proceedings of the Twenty-Eighth Congress*. Vol. XIV.

U.S. Dept. of Commerce. Eighth Decennial Census (1860). U.S. Slave Schedule. Washington, D.C.: National Archives and Records Administration, 1860. M653, 1,438 rolls.

U.S. Government. *Annual Report of the Commissioner of the General Land Office.* Washington, D.C., 1887.

————. *Biographical Directory of the United States Congress.* N.p., n.d.

U.S. National Park Service. Cane River National Heritage Area: Cherokee Plantation.

————. "Myrtles Plantation." www.nps.gov/nr/travel/louisiana/myr.htm.

————. "NPS Soldiers and Sailors System." www.nps.gov/civilwar/search-soldiers. htm, M378 ROLL 18.

Vlach, John Michael. *Back of the Big House: The Architecture of Plantation Slavery.* Chapel Hill: University of North Carolina Press, 1993.

Whitehead, Thomas N. Personal communication, January 6, 2017.

Williams, Jack K. *Dueling in the Old South: Vignettes of Social History.* College Station: Texas A&M University Press, 1980.

Wilson, Samuel, Jr. "Nomination Form: Melrose Plantation." National Register of Historic Places, National Park Service, 1972.

About the Authors

William Ryan Smith holds a master of arts degree in heritage resources from Northwestern State University in Natchitoches, Louisiana, and works in healthcare administration. He makes his home in Shreveport with his wife, Leslie, and three sons, William, Jack and Colin. This is his first work with The History Press.

Cheryl H. White is an associate professor of history at Louisiana State University at Shreveport, where she teaches medieval and early modern European history. She also has a great interest in the local and regional history of her home state. She has authored four other titles with The History Press and has written or edited several other historical works for other academic presses and journals.

Visit us at
www.historypress.net

....

This title is also available as an e-book